REDEFINING HRM- DELIVER VALUE IN THIS EVER CHANGING WORLD!

HOW CAN HUMAN CAPITAL BE HARNESSED AND LINKED TO BUSINESS STRATEGY, PERFORMANCE, AND GROWTH?

DR. AMIT DAS

To

All my bosses and mentors who made a difference in my professional career.

"The market for consultants, motivators, and trainers that increase employees' productivity is quite significant. There are a tonne of books that have been published about employee performance and engagement. Even with all of these resources at their disposal, far too many businesses still fail to achieve the greatest possible output from their employees. There appear to be unhappy employees around who struggle with workplace depression all the time. They persist because they need a job and a source of money. It's not necessary to be that way."

- Dr. Amit Das, Motivational Speaker, Leadership Coach , Counsellor, and Mentor.

Contents

Foreword ...... *vii*

Preface ...... *xiii*

Acknowledgements ...... *xix*

1. Need To Focus More On People Than Processes 1

2. Cultivating A Happier And Productive Work Environment 76

3. Forecast Outcomes With A High Degree Of Certainty 133

References 165

About The Author 169

Foreword

Dear Reader,

Thank you for taking the time to learn more about HRM and HR's critical functions in an organisation that is constantly delivering value in this ever changing world. By reading this book, you will learn more about employee happiness and the rewarding outcome of increased employee productivity.

This book explains how to utilise technology to make your HR operations more efficient. The author outlines the processes for streamlining routine activities, including onboarding, scheduling, payroll, reporting, compliance, and communication, while walking you through every stage of the HR workflow.

This book is a turning point for the HR industry since it discusses how to find the most relevant sources of data, gather information in a transparent manner that complies with data protection laws, and transform that data into actionable insights.

The author shows exactly how to choose, implement, and use metrics to improve decision-making, optimise organisational effectiveness, and maximise the value of HR investments.

"Organisations with a greater chance of success are those who cherish their employees and show them that they care."

Over the past two years, there have been significant changes in the way you work, and this is only the beginning. An important development is the rise in concern for employees' general wellbeing and mental health. This change is significant and, hopefully, will last into the future.

You are frequently left wondering how to establish a culture where workers are content and fulfilled in their jobs as organisations grow more sensitive to their requirements and as people become more outspoken about their wants. Although management may think they have everything under control, the outcomes are frequently high turnover, low productivity, and subpar customer service.

HR must quickly adjust in these times of change and upheaval. This book offers the solutions needed to ensure that all facets of the human resource operate to their greatest potential. Redefining HRM offers a novel perspective on how human resources should have been developed. HR is in a unique position to make use of a variety of other intangibles as well, including organisational goodwill, intellectual capital, collaborative knowledge, and research and analytics.

Dr. Amit Das, the author of "Redefining HRM" discovered that emotions have a persistent impact on you as people. Emotional responses to situations can lead to both happiness and misery. People wish to stay in happy places because they like to be happy.

"Happiness encourages excellence, and when a business fosters a culture of happiness that leads to a joyful workplace, the chances for both business success and employee success may dramatically increase."

The author Dr. Amit Das has 25 years of experience working with both employees and employers as a consultant, and speaker. He has tested and refined these shift-producing techniques over the course of that period on a variety of topics, including time management, decision-making, setting goals, and being extraordinary at workplace.

While reading this book, you will go on a journey exploring why and how leaders should develop into compassionate capitalists and make sure that their employees are successful in unlocking happiness at work.

This book, "Redefining HRM," dispels the fallacy that workplace happiness is a waste of time and shows how it may result in a more engaged and productive workforce, which can really affect the bottom line.

"Agility is a crucial component of doing business in the modern workplace."

This is a helpfull book on developing agile procedures and practises for the HR function that will save time, improve performance, and support overarching business objectives. It is designed expressly for working professionals. Whether they are giant traditional corporations or tiny tech start-ups, businesses need to be quick, adaptable, and digitally enabled to flourish.

This book, "Redefining HRM," is a fundamental manual for all HR professionals who want to make their HR practises flexible and improve business performance but are unsure where to begin. It covers every aspect of the HR function, from people processes, ways of working, and HR services to organisation design, operating models, and HR teams.

"There are many reasons you choose an occupation, which includes a passion for work. Whatever the motivation, finding contentment and satisfaction in your everyday activities may have a great impact on your lifestyle as a whole and enhance your productivity at work.
"

For HR professionals, people leaders, and business executives, it offers a practical framework of cutting-edge concepts and methods. It is a comprehensive reference to the core elements of contemporary HR. This is not a theoretical analysis of human resources. This book is written for practitioners and features the opinions of human resources leaders from organisations.

There is priceless advice on how HR can effectively prioritise and determine which activities to pursue, which to develop, which to rework, and which to abandon in order to achieve continuous business improvement, in addition to advice on how to deal with resistance, manage a backlog, and deal with constraints. This is an essential reading for all HR professionals in organisations of any size that must adopt quick, flexible, and evolving flexible approaches in order to successfully compete in the new world of work.

This book, "Redefining HRM," is about using positive psychology at work that is surprisingly useful and easy to read. Start here if you're looking for something more motivating and significant than employee engagement. The author Dr. Amit Das wants to make workplace a happier place.

You'll deepen team involvement and position your team for success if you heed his realistic and inspiring advice. The techniques in this book will assist you in building better ties, finding more energy, and radiating more pleasant emotions.

This book, "Redefining HRM," will be a priceless resource for corporate leaders who want greater value from HR; HR professionals planning analytics projects; and HR executives setting up or heading analytics divisions.

This is a rewarding book for employers, managers, company owners, consultants, and other people in charge of leading teams to succeed in a competitive environment. Its low-and no-cost strategies are taken from hundreds of businesses around the world. They have been modified to meet the needs of an evolving workplace, particularly to deal creatively with virtual employees, freelancers, international coworkers, and the rule-bending expectations of employees.

This book, written by Dr. Amit Das, reveals fresh viewpoints and strategies for rethinking hiring, employees management, performance, and rewards to save time, cut costs, and increase company success. It covers important HR strategies including diversity and inclusion, people analytics, learning and development (L&D), and employee experience. For all HR practitioners and company executives looking to build a world-class people management department, "Redefining HRM" is a vital resource.

This book, "Redefining HRM," gives a way to work engagement, sure, but it also offers something larger and more powerful than engagement alone. Use this book to put happiness to work to benefit you and your team.

"Too many businesses, however, are constrained by compliance-driven, segregated HR practises that hinder rather than help the business."

Thank you for taking the time to read this book.

So, happy reading and learning to all my readers.

Carpe diem.

Dr. Amit Das

Motivational Speaker, Leadership Coach, Counsellor, and Mentor.

Preface

"A business that lost all of its equipment but still had its employees might resume operations rather soon. A business that lost its best employees but kept its assets would never be able to recover."

The function of HR has seen significant changes in recent decades. In the past, managers have seen the role of human resources as purely administrative and professional. The HR team didn't view itself as contributing to the organisation's overarching strategy; instead, they were primarily concerned with managing benefits and other payroll and operational tasks. Even while top-line managers and human resource specialists are aware of this potential, many of them are unsure of how to start the process of achieving it.

More than ever, HR professionals need to provide scientific evidence of a direct connection between their actions and company success. I will provide you effective techniques for peeping inside the HR "black box," implementing human capital metrics that track the efficacy of talent policies and practises, demonstrating the logical connections to financial and line-of-business metrics, and using HR metrics to drive more effective decision-making.

"Your work is going to fill a large part of your life, and the only way to be truly satisfied is to do what you believe is great work. And the only way to do great work is to love what you do. If you haven't found it yet, keep looking. Don't settle."- Steve Jobs

It is more important than ever for HR professionals to comprehend and use data analytics. Successful HR professionals of today must ask insightful questions, comprehend important concepts, and use data in an intelligent manner, but they may not fully comprehend the many forms, types, applications, interpretations, and capabilities of HR analytics.

Businesses have been preoccupied with talent for the past ten or twelve years. The continuous talent battle grew more competitive in 2021 as companies dealt with the "Great Resignation", in which workers willingly quit secure employment in large numbers. Businesses that want to stand out in today's globalised and fiercely competitive business environment feel compelled to implement management strategies that incorporate behavioural traits that can foster workplace pleasure, which supports both individual growth and organisational competitiveness.

"Employee satisfaction is important in a corporate environment that is becoming more and more characterised by values."

It is difficult to turn the enormous promise of people analytics into reality. Important insights from pioneering practitioners can help you succeed. Their experiences—as well as their priceless insights—are shared in this book.

I will assist you in bringing focus and clarity to any workforce analytics project with solid research design and analysis to obtain trustworthy insights. I will provide information on where to begin, how to get stakeholder support, and how to achieve "early wins" that may be built upon.

A new phenomenon called the "Era of Employee Satisfaction" has emerged as a result of the growing importance of "Employees' Job Experience," which places a strong emphasis on individuality, purpose, and choice. Being content at work wasn't a big concern not so long ago. The most skilled and promising individuals are more likely to move on to greater possibilities. People must execute to the best of their ability for organisations to preserve their competitive edge.

However, it has never been more challenging to assist and grow people in a world of rising stress and pressure, fast technological development, and digital overload. It is obvious that having content employees is a requirement for every successful workplace. Productivity, motivation, dedication, and retention all depend on it.

How frequently, as an employer, have you given thought to your workers' happiness at work and taken action to make them happy?

You can claim that in order to assure employee happiness, your organisation held employee engagement events and conducted employee satisfaction surveys. The fact that different people perceive happiness in various ways is one explanation for this. Not just feeling happy all the time qualifies as employee happiness. It involves approaching one's work with optimism, being willing to work through issues rather than whine, taking helpful criticism, and continuously striving to get better without feeling pressured.

It is therefore basic and critical that it be recognised as an integral component of human pleasure. As a result, it is crucial that employees feel extremely happy and appreciated in the workplaces where they work. The observation of unfavourable and unwelcome conduct that resulted in the employee's performance declining, such as a lack of commitment to the organisation and the role to play, gave rise to the concept of workplace happiness.

All of this research data claims that the solution is straightforward by keeping your employees content because their contentment will boost organisational efficiency. It doesn't operate that way in practice. These initiatives might not, however, ensure the anticipated outcomes.

As you can see, contented employees are productive employees. You must make sure that your employees are happy with their positions as managers. This will make it possible for your team to accomplish its goals, go above and beyond, and support the organisation in trying circumstances.

Having contented employees has a lot of benefits for the company. When your employees are content, you will also be satisfied. A content employee works hard and accomplishes their objectives.

"Most crucially, content workers are more ready to balance their own goals with overarching company goals. They also promote a more welcoming and cooperative work atmosphere, assist in strengthening connections within the team, and provide clients with more cordial service."

However, employee happiness cannot be boiled down to witty statistics and figures. Even though you might not realise it, being sad has a tremendous impact on everything you do. It seriously lowers your performance. Although the connection between contentment and productivity is not new, many businesses continue to undervalue its significance in the workplace.

"HR architecture may be the difference between an organisation that is merely keeping up with the competition and one that is ahead of it with the correct mentality and measuring tools."

HR practitioners must create and incorporate employee experience throughout an organisation's procedures and culture—from the minute an employee views a job advertisement to the moment they leave the organisation—in order to generate top-performing workers.

This book, "Redefining HRM," is packed with resources, suggestions, and guidance to assist HR professionals and company executives in inspiring, fostering, and developing their workforce to achieve great individual and organisational results. It offers advice on how to use networks, nudges, and technology to communicate, sustain, and evolve employee contentment. It also covers how to establish happiness competencies in an HR organisation. Each tip's methodology and justification are detailed in detail. The advantages and outcomes that can be attained by straightforward adjustments and actions are illustrated in real-world workplace stories.

With the knowledge gained from using these skills, you'll be able to behave, feel, and think in ways that lead to purpose, success, and happiness regardless of the situation. By studying examples from real-world settings, you will learn how to identify the best candidates for a position and hire the best candidate. When the applicant is hired, you'll learn how to help your new employee adjust to the workplace and promote excellence.

Uninspired workers lead to terrible performance and a lot of turnover. Your human resource managers should make solving these issues their top priority, but they don't have the time because they are busy with paperwork most of the time.

"Workers who are happy are more productive and show their true potential."

Managers throughout the organisation can comprehend precisely how people may produce value and how to monitor the value-creation process with the help of a properly built strategic HR architecture.

When you make the necessary modifications, you'll learn how to do it and, even better, you'll see what the employee experience is like. Your greatest asset is people. Putting the tactics described in this book into practise can improve your capacity to draw in and keep people, providing you with a competitive edge.

HR is now ideally positioned to leverage corporate data to drive performance, both of the individuals in the organisation and the organisation as a whole. HR was traditionally thought of as a purely human job, uninterested in numbers. Data-Driven HR is a useful manual that teaches HR professionals how to make the most of the wealth of data at their disposal.

Through the use of technology, partnerships, best practises in data management, and skill development, you'll discover how to maintain success. Last but not least, you'll learn how to add even more value by fostering an analytical attitude throughout HR and honing two crucial abilities: narrative and visualisation.

This book examines how data can contribute to organisational success by, among other things, optimising processes, driving performance, and improving HR decision-making. It covers all the essential components of HR, including recruitment, employee engagement, performance management, wellbeing, and training. This is required reading for all HR professionals aiming to make a demonstrable difference in their businesses since it is filled with case studies and real-world examples.

"You must relieve HR of the weight of tedious, soul-crushing processes if you want to treat your employees and the clients they serve fairly."

Acknowledgements

At the outset, I will thank my family for supporting me throughout the journey of writing my book and encouraging me to live my dreams; my son has always been instrumental in giving his inspiration to complete the writing of this book. Despite the fact that I am listed as the author of this book, **"Redefining HRM- Deliver Value In This Ever Changing World!"** *would not have been published if I had depended entirely on my own talents. Creating this book required more than anything—it took a family of dedicated and caring people who were always prepared to lend a hand.*

Writing a book while working full-time is no simple task, so I'd want to express my gratitude to my amazing coworkers who act as cheerleaders in equal measure. Thank you, too, to my students and clients for your patience and unflinching support while I worked on this book!

Thank you to everyone who has listened to me argue for doing everything you can to make your life, including your work life, more progressive. I appreciate everyone's assistance throughout the process. This book would not have been possible without each of you having had an impact on my life in some manner.

Lastly, I would like to thank all the people with whom I have been associated. You gave me power. I would like to thank Notion Press for publishing my book. Finally, thank you all for gifting your time to read this book.

I'd want to convey my heartfelt appreciation to the almighty God for bestowing his blessings and being so gracious.

CHAPTER ONE

Need To Focus More On People Than Processes

"HR managers must come back to the basics by engaging leaders and employees in meaningful conversations. Any app or AI won't be able to replace a real-world conversation and the emotions within it."

An organisation must constantly sharpen its competitive edge if it wants to maintain and improve its commercial success. This endeavour has traditionally been accomplished by entry obstacles at the industry level, patent protection, and governmental rules. But those obstacles have mostly been removed as a result of fast technological advancement, innovation, and deregulation. Competitive advantage today comes primarily from the internal resources and capabilities of individual organisations, including a organisation's ability to develop and retain a capable and committed workforce, because long-lasting, superior performance now demands flexibility, innovation, and speed to market.

The "employee contentment" concept goes beyond mere catchphrases.

Unmistakable evidence suggests that the growing strategic potential of human resources depends on the economy's rising emphasis on intangible assets and intellectual capital. Intangible resources like brand recognition, expertise, innovation, and, in particular, human capital, are essential for gaining a competitive advantage in the new economy. Business executives must thus respond to the challenge by integrating the HR function into the entire corporate strategy of the organisation. Creating a measuring system that effectively illustrates HR's impact on organisation success is the most effective step HR managers can take to ensure their strategic contribution.

"Making informed business decisions requires having access to a wealth of information, and HR metrics and organisational people-related statistics are a priceless source of such knowledge. But in order to effectively utilise the potential of this data, HR practitioners frequently lack the statistical and analytical skills necessary."

Senior managers view employees as strategic assets, but they don't make investments to improve HR's skills. As a result, the HR system is unable to benefit from management's viewpoint. The high-performance viewpoint HR and other executives see HR as an integral part of the bigger system for implementing the organisation's goal. The business oversees and monitors the interaction between these two systems and overall business performance.

To assure their strategic contribution, HR managers should, in my opinion, build a measuring system that demonstrates HR's influence on company performance.

HR managers must take a fundamentally new viewpoint when designing such a measuring system, one that focuses on how human resources can be a key component of carrying out the organisation's strategy.

How can HR professionals objectively evaluate their present procedures and endeavours in order to pinpoint the places where they need to adopt new perspectives in order to generate commercial results?

Employee contentment has been defined in a variety of ways, from the succinct and direct to the descriptive and in-depth. Numerous aspects of an employee's loyalty to the company or the admirable traits that an engaged employee demonstrates are emphasised in these descriptions. Examples of definitions for employee involvement include:

- Employee contentment is the degree of the psychological and emotional attachment workers have to their workplaces.
- Employees who are active with, passionate about, and devoted to their work and workplace are defined as being "engaged" by Gallup.
- At Willis Watson, "Employee Contentment" refers to their desire and capacity to contribute to the success of the organisation.
- Employee contentment, according to Aon Hewitt, refers to "the degree of an employee's psychological involvement in their firm."

Employee dedication and connection to an organisation is measured by the phrase "employee happiness or satisfaction." In today's cutthroat corporate environment, employee contentment has emerged as a crucial success factor. High levels of job satisfaction enhance shareholder value, build consumer loyalty, and help organisations retain their best employees. The "employee contentment" concept goes beyond mere catchphrases. It's a cornerstone of sensible business. Additionally, all businesses desire to raise employee job satisfaction. Numerous studies have shown that organisations with higher levels of employee contentment perform better.

Did you know, however, that fewer than 33% of all workers are totally engaged, which is to say, they are dedicated, driven, and emotionally invested in the business?

I work with many HR executives who are interested in learning the formula for raising employee contentment in a way that boosts the bottom line. I will now share this methodology with you. Leaders emphasize contentment primarily in order to get people to exert that enchanted fairy dust known as discretionary effort. The difference between having to do something and wanting to do it is discretionary effort. Going above and beyond what is required by the job description is key. Leaders adore the concept of discretionary effort because it boosts output and revenue with no additional expense. However, the kinds of efforts that are favoured by various businesses may differ.

Do you consider working extra hours, putting in long hours each week, missing lunch, checking emails over the weekend, or being patient with a difficult customer?

Aiding a struggling team, putting in unrequested extra time, offering a cost-cutting suggestion, or buying a busy boss takeout for lunch? You must ensure that any discussion of discretionary effort is consistent with the culture and values of the organisation. Discretionary effort has its limitations, even if it is typically a desirable thing. Overwork can result in fatigue, tension, burnout, and resentment. The reality is that various employees have varying levels of capability for involvement. You'll discover that keeping a balance between your employees' involvement and discretionary effort is important. Pushing too hard will result in dissatisfaction; pushing too little will lead to mediocrity.

Of course, a person's innate lethargy, distractions from other things on their plate, general indifference, a bad match, and other conflicting interests can all reduce their discretionary effort, even in a favourable situation. Imagine a department that is already quite productive.

Do you really need to worry about how engaged your employees are in that circumstance?

You do, of course. Increased involvement results in increased profitability, productivity, innovation, reduced attrition, and reduced risk of claims. The phrases "work satisfaction" and "contentment" are sometimes used interchangeably. The determinants of contentment and satisfaction do, however, have certain similarities, according to studies, but there are also important distinctions between the factors that make up each one.

According to some experts, contentment is defined in terms of employees' emotions and actions. Employees who are engaged with their job may say they feel deeply immersed and concentrated. They have a sense of urgency and are excited. Engaged conduct is tenacious, pro-active, and adaptable in ways that, if needed, broaden the work tasks. Employee contentment goes beyond responsibilities in areas like service delivery or innovation. Satisfied workers, in comparison, feel nice, comfortable, and fulfilled.

Engaged employees, on the other hand, feel focused with a feeling of urgency and concentrate on how they approach what they do. In contrast to employee contentment levels, which are generally under the direct control of or considerably impacted by the employee's boss, employee job satisfaction in an organisation frequently correlates to elements that the business has control over (such as compensation, benefits, and job security) (through job assignments, trust, recognition, day-to-day communications, etc.). After analyzing 840,000 employee contentment answers from businesses in the U.S. and Britain, researchers at the Kenexa High Performance Institute discovered that 57% of respondents were disengaged after two years on the job.

Where do you find major challenges with employees' contentment?

Increasing employee contentment is one of the top five worldwide company initiatives, according to executives from around the world. Employees' contentment is a critical factor in customer satisfaction, brand reputation, and shareholder value. It also has the ability to have a substantial impact on employees retention, productivity, and loyalty. Organisations are increasingly looking to HR to determine the direction of employee commitment and contentment in order to gain a competitive edge. The majority of CEOs are already aware that employee contentment has a direct impact on the stability and profitability of a firm. Only 33% of American workers, according to Gallup, are engaged in their work. The majority of businesses still have a lot of work to do in order to realise the full potential of their workforce because 52% of employees claim to be "simply showing up" and 17% identify as "actively disengaged."

A few adjectives that best represent millennial talent are passion, spontaneity, boldness, digital savvy, agility, risk-taking, and catalysts of change. Millennials already make up the bulk of the global workforce, and by 2025, it's predicted that they will make up 75% of all workers. In order to create a workplace that is suitable for the future and to maintain a productive workforce, it is becoming increasingly important to successfully attract, develop, and retain millennial talent.

Because engaged employees do better work, employee contentment has always been a top concern for businesses of all sizes and across all sectors. Maintaining employee contentment has never been more crucial than it is now, when employees are more dispersed and separated from one another than ever before, there is a breaking international news story to read about every few minutes, and everyone is wondering when they'll wake up to a normal world once more. Across the world, 85% of workers are either not engaged or actively disengaged at work. It's also obvious that low employee contentment affects more than just your business culture; it also has an effect on your financial line, with companies in the top quartile of employee contentment reporting 21% better profitability than those in the worst quartile. Higher levels of employee contentment have also been linked to:

- It reduces turnover while increasing retention.
- Develop more original concepts.
- Increasing client and customer satisfaction.
- Increase productivity at work.
- It makes for more wholesome workers.

The leadership and people management teams may start the process of developing workplace rules and initiatives that encourage deeper, more meaningful involvement for all workers once they have a better understanding of the corporate culture. Social cohesiveness, feeling supported by one's boss, information sharing, shared objectives and vision, communication, and trust may all have an impact on contentment and productivity. Employees want to be appreciated and valued; they want to know that their work matters and that their opinions are taken seriously. Employees that are highly engaged are more dedicated to their employers and more productive.

The following principles should be taken into account by organisations when creating employee contentment surveys:

- Employee contentment motivations differ not just from nation to nation but also by industrial sector and within businesses. As a result, businesses that are growing internationally need to understand what motivates their employees in various international regions.
- Employers who want to engage their workforce worldwide should consider international HR choices in light of national cultural norms.
- To match HR policies for a local community with actual employee attitudes and views, use accurate research rather than preconceptions.
- To properly understand employee surveys, it is essential to examine data on national norms because the standard for involvement differs greatly from country to country.
- Recognise that the components of contentment also contribute to the employment brand. Recognise that the corporate culture is reflected in the way the organisation does its business.
- You are aware that asking your workers directly is the best approach to find out if they are interested in their

work. Example: Last year, you were honoured to receive recognition from Inc. Best Workplaces for your corporate culture, but more importantly, you were gratified to have been selected based on the combined experiences of your workers. So, how do you begin to create a stimulating work environment for your teams? Take your example and begin with the people. Your workers will feel appreciated when you make an effort to connect with them and start a conversation about how you can best assist them, and you'll be on your way to establishing an atmosphere where everyone feels more involved and, yes, happier, too.

- One of those concepts that might be challenging to define is employee contentment. The only employees that complete their tasks on time are those who are happy. Are happy workers those that frequently speak out during team meetings? It may be challenging to determine whether your workers are genuinely interested in their job or are merely scraping by on a daily basis because there are so many different corporate cultures and sectors out there, all with differing measures to assess success. In the end, when it comes to assessing the level of employee contentment at your own business, you'll only know it when you see it.

What are those predominant HR factors that can influence employees' contentment?

Your HR department will be necessary if you want to fully transform employee happiness at your business. Your organisation's human resources department will need your assistance in developing enduring company-wide happiness initiatives for your employees. Specifically, they will need the results of the happiness surveys mentioned earlier. It can take a long time to develop happiness programs that resonate with all of your employees, regardless of where they work or how long they have been at your organisation.

In order to promote a stronger connection between individual workers and the company as a whole, one of the most popular happiness programs for hybrid organisations is to establish a shared objective that the whole workforce of your organisation can strive toward together. This will help encourage a stronger bond between each employee and your business. Pick a target that aligns with your mission statement and can be accomplished by hybrid personnel that work both in-person and remotely.

- Employee motivation is the responsibility of management and human resources procedures that might boost contentment. HR must standardize guidelines for creating activities and surveys that will increase employee contentment.
- As HR professionals think about implementing or changing procedures or programs to raise employee contentment, they have to: Make wise investing decisions.
- In order to increase contentment levels, the firm should evaluate the strategic implications of different HR practices and decide which are more crucial and warrant higher investment.
- HR specialists should be able to show how these investments have produced profitable, quantifiable business results for their firm or other companies.
- Numerous elements, including workplace culture, organisational communication, and management approaches, as well as trust and respect, leadership, and

firm reputation, have an impact on employee contentment.

- Managers and HR specialists are crucial to the success of the company's employee contentment activities, both collectively and individually.
- Think about the unanticipated effects. Consider the expected effect of the altered rules while assessing choices for restructuring HR procedures to promote employee contentment.
- Are there any possibly unforeseen, undesirable effects that might arise depending on how that modification affects employees in various scenarios and life situations? Make informed investing decisions.
- Every year, employee contentment should be evaluated. The major performance indicators for the company, such as profitability, productivity, quality, customer happiness, and customer loyalty, should be connected to survey questions. Finding the most effective contentment levers and survey questions that distinguish the best-performing business units from less successful ones should be among the results of employee contentment research.
- HR should take the lead in developing proactive workplace policies and practices that help recruit and retain individuals with the skills and competencies required for development and sustainability in order to build a culture of contentment.
- Opportunities for communication and techniques for involving employees improve their contentment level.
- Utilise pay-for-performance schemes to draw employees' attention to desired actions. Adopt competency-based compensation to promote knowledge and skill acquisition and improve employee

performance.

- Establish tough targets that are in line with the strategic goals of the organisation, offer feedback, and acknowledge successes and more volunteer efforts.
- Targeted communication activities may help managers and HR specialists monitor employee contentment concerns, collect regular employee input, and foresee how workgroup requirements will change over time. Managers and HR specialists should seize opportunities to engage staff members and should do so by using a variety of communication channels. Improving contentment starts with understanding its cause.

The sort of communication used for contentment activities should be determined by the size, makeup, and anticipated response of the target group of employees. Regular weekly or biweekly meetings can be used to maintain contact with workgroups; ideally, 15 to 20 people should attend each meeting. To get prompt feedback, concerns or suggestions can be shared in this thread. One-on-one conversations with a worker targeted for exceptional performance, recognised for performance development, or randomly selected from the workgroup are another element of staying in contact. The sort of communication used for contentment activities should be determined by the size, makeup, and anticipated response of the target group of employees. HR professionals and managers can use the following communication techniques:

- Remote interaction Managers and HR professionals may communicate through a variety of technologies, such as employee listening platforms where HR can poll employees, collect feedback, conduct departure interviews, etc.

- Social media and smartphone apps are tools for conducting surveys, exchanging ideas, and voting on problems.
- The blogs that regularly update staff members on new projects and enable the recording and public release of their comments.
- Teleconferences and videoconferences electronic newsletters.
- Include inquiries that could be made annually or more frequently. For the management of employee contentment, this will serve as a baseline. Good inquiries delve into the routine actions of managers and staff members and, whenever feasible, connect those actions to customer service.
- Use positive or neutral words. Change the question from "Are there too many employees for a company your size?" to "Is your line-to-employee ratio appropriate for a company your size?" Negative language should be avoided.
- Avoid asking ambiguous or misleading questions. For instance, even among motivated employees, inquiries like "Do you look forward to going to work on Mondays?" are likely to elicit a "no" response.
- Make sure the survey is not too long. Long surveys have a lower response rate and may provide biased results because respondents become bored. Surveys that are too lengthy discourage respondents and may provide biased results as people review their answers in an effort to complete the survey as soon as feasible.
- If you engage with a vendor that approaches you with a "typical" list of questions, think about customising the list of questions to fit the needs of your organisation.

- When you distribute the questionnaire, take into account what you're stating about the organisation's ideals. The choice of questions is important since it communicates to employees what the company cares enough to inquire about.
- Employers frequently have the opportunity to inspire and instruct workers at "engageable moments."

Many organisations undertake workforce surveys to gauge employee contentment levels inside the company and to examine the connections between employee contentment and important business outcomes. These polls' findings can show which contentment activities are succeeding in attaining their objectives. Employee contentment may be measured through surveys, but employers must understand that these surveys are different from conventional employee surveys. Surveys of employee contentment differ from other employee surveys in their focus. An employee culture survey evaluates employees' perspectives, whereas employee opinion and satisfaction surveys gauge employees' opinions, attitudes, and impressions of their company.

"The pandemic has really empowered us to speak for ourselves in a lot of things. How do we leverage qualitative analytics to a greater degree? How do we encourage people to provide insight that you wouldn't get through data?"
-Renee Ovrut, MUFG Union Bank

To enable individual managers to make adjustments that will really improve contentment levels, survey data should be examined in aggregate and broken down for each business unit once it has been administered. Additionally, some authorities advise having line managers make action plans to implement survey suggestions and disseminate survey results to their own staff. Additionally, the company may mandate that all workers include contentment goals in their performance evaluations so that contentment targets can be created both top-down and bottom-up. Make sure management informs workers that the survey is an organisational activity rather than a PR campaign.

- Create a survey committee if you want to get widespread support.
- Conduct feedback sessions or focus groups to ascertain the level of relevance of certain survey items.
- To guarantee that improvements are made based on employee feedback, involve the whole management team in the action-planning process.
- To protect survey input anonymity, organise open-ended survey responses by theme and classify them at the workgroup level.

Request some written feedback. Some businesses include open-ended questions at the end of surveys so that workers may leave feedback in order to identify any topics they may have missed and that they might wish to cover in the future. Think about doing many different survey types, each with unique questions, frequencies, and audiences. For instance, "pulse" surveys, which are shorter, more frequent surveys that address certain concerns or are sent to particular workforce groups, might be conducted in between yearly surveys. You might also carry out different surveys among firm executives and staff, or in other business divisions or regions.

- Platforms for employee contentment, more than just feedback tools

- A new world of employee contentment measurement tools
- Calculating the return on employee investment
- Accessing contentment research

Contentment surveys measure employees' commitment, motivation, sense of purpose, and passion for their work and the organisation. Employee opinion and satisfaction surveys measure workers' views, attitudes, and perceptions of their organisation. An employee culture survey measures employees' points of view to assess whether they align with the organisation or its departments.

Employee Contentment or Satisfaction Surveys: Why do employees lack trust in them?

Ensure the employee satisfaction survey is carefully crafted. Employers should develop a comprehensive contentment plan that goes beyond merely tracking contentment ratings if they want to get the greatest results. A plan for employee contentment should ideally be developed prior to conducting a contentment survey. These five elements will be included in an efficient plan:

- How the plan will be explained?
- How to identify the action areas?
- What quantifiable results will be used to gauge development?
- What particular steps will be taken in response to the survey results?
- How will be the long-term sustainability of the contentment approach achieved?

People quit managers, not organisations, according to studies, so it is crucial for managers to actively manage employee contentment. But middle managers must be given additional authority through the extension of their tasks, training for these new responsibilities, and more participation in strategic choices. In order to hold managers responsible for the levels of contentment, an organisation's leaders and HR experts should:

- Ensure that managers and workers have the resources they need to do their duties effectively.
- Give managers progressively bigger and more interesting duties.
- Give managers the right level of power.
- Intensify efforts to cultivate leaders.

Do you understand how much your employees are engaged in their respective assignments?

Employees are categorised by organisations that undertake research on employee contentment according to the amount of involvement, although they do it using various nomenclature. Employees who are involved and those who are not totally engaged, for instance, have been described as: "Actively engaged" (loyal and productive), "not engaged" (average performance), and "actively disengaged" are differentiated by Gallup ("retired on active duty").

"Employees who are "engaged" (know what to do and want to do it) are distinguished from "disengaged" (know what to do but don't want to do it), "enthusiasts" (who want to do the work but don't know how to do it), and "renegades" (those who know what to do but do not want to do it). Disengaged workers typically perform the bare minimum and have no meaningful connection to their work. Discontentment may manifest in a variety of typical ways, such as a rapid shift toward a 9-to-5 time clock mentality, a reluctance to engage in social activities outside of the workplace, or a propensity to isolate oneself from peers. It is most noticeable when a normally vivacious and energetic person fades away and offers nothing constructive. They could dislike their occupations, have a habit of complaining to coworkers, and lower productivity levels.

How do you deal with disengaged workers in order to foster a happy workplace?

First, spend some time figuring out why your team members aren't as invested in the project as normal. Honesty, openness, and appreciation are the foundations of effective employee contentment. When you are proud of the organisation you work for, you are more likely to be proud of the work you perform. Similar to this, there is a higher likelihood that employees will become disengaged with the task they are doing if they spend the whole day creating work that neither their peers nor superiors notice. Making your company a place where everyone is glad to work and where all workers are recognised for their dedication is the first step toward full employee contentment.

Employee contentment behaviors

- They are engaged in their actions.
- They are optimistic.
- They are team-oriented.
- They surpass all expectations.
- They are solution-oriented.
- They are selfless.

- They demonstrate a desire to learn.
- They transfer credit while acknowledging their fault.

Employee dissatisfaction behaviors

- They are disinterested in their actions.
- They are pessimistic.
- They are self-centered.
- Their absence rate is high.
- They demonstrate negative attitude.
- They are egocentric.
- They Emphasise monetary value.
- They take credit but transfers blame.

Only 26% of executives polled by Dale Carnegie in 2017 stated that employee satisfaction is a very important factor in their daily decisions, plans, and actions. The rest just work on it occasionally, seldom, or never, according to another 42% of respondents. Some studies pinpoint the organisational-wide factors that influence employee contentment. Few factors that have the biggest influence on employee contentment, according to the research company behind the "Best Places to Work" programs in more than 47 metro regions, are as follows:

- Their organisation's executives are dedicated to making it a terrific place to work.
- Put their faith in the organisation's leaders to steer it in the correct direction.
- Confidence in the future prosperity of the company.
- Knowledge about organisation's future goals.
- People are the most valuable resource to the organisation's leaders.

- The company makes investments to increase employee success.

When employees have great experiences on a regular basis, employee contentment grows tremendously. When employees have pleasant interactions with their immediate managers or supervisors on a regular basis, employee contentment rises significantly. The following actions of a direct supervisor have been linked to employee contentment:

Factors that are important and closely related to important business outcomes. These factors have to do with what an employee receives (such as clear expectations and resources), what an employee gives (such as individual contributions), whether an employee fits into the organisation (such as based on the organisation's mission and coworkers), and whether the employee has the chance to advance (e.g., by getting feedback about work and opportunities to learn).

- Employees are equipped with all they need to accomplish their jobs properly.
- The relationship between employees and their boss is positive.
- Employees have the power they need to do their jobs properly.
- Employees have the autonomy to choose their jobs.
- By building a respectful and trustworthy relationship with their direct reports, articulating company values, and establishing expectations for the day-to-day operations of any organisation, middle managers play a critical role in employee contentment.

- Assist in the transformation of the company by asking management to communicate the business purpose and vision.
- Employers should carefully consider the design of contentment programs if they want to raise employee contentment levels.
- Emphasising the importance of contentment in the mission statement and executive communications; making sure that business units carry out their contentment action plans; keeping track of progress; making necessary adjustments to strategies and plans; and acknowledging and celebrating accomplishments.
- Employee contentment is significantly impacted by HR procedures. Jobs and tasks should have significance, variety, autonomy, and respect for coworkers so that employees will perceive their roles more widely and be more inclined to take on responsibilities outside of their job descriptions.
- Recruiting Look for candidates who will find their work fascinating and challenging. Encourage people to withdraw from the process if they are not suitable for a certain job.
- Select applicants who are most likely to carry out their work responsibilities successfully, offer their time voluntarily, and behave appropriately.
- Give an orientation to help people understand how their work fits within the company. In order to improve job performance, contentment, and self-efficacy, provide skill development training.

When a young person first enters the workforce, certain factors might make selecting a professional path difficult, if not impossible. The small whispers in the back of your thoughts quickly pull you back to your everyday realities, even if you are bold enough to envision an admirable objective for your future selves. The voice that is the loudest among them all wants to discuss only one subject: money. Almost everyone has received well-intentioned family advice to select a wealthy job in order to have a happy future. I use the word "well-meaning" because the person offering the advice, who is frequently a parent or grandmother, genuinely wishes to spare you from a life of stress and difficulty.

"Early in my career, one of the first business lessons I learned was this: It's impossible to win the hearts and minds of people unless you clearly establish goals and values and reward people if they act in a way that leads to the fulfillment of those objectives. It quickly became clear to me that if you want to make sure your customers are treated well, you have to make sure you treat your employees well and recognize their efforts." - F. Robert Salerno, CEO of Avis

Alternatively, it's possible that your own inner voice is advising you to pursue a job path that will pay you more money, citing the growing cost of living or the need to pay back college loans. Nobody likes to think of living in a world where money is a major issue, so even if the job doesn't make you happy, it might be tempting to choose one that pays well in order to escape that battle.

"Only focusing on perks is no longer sufficient to retain competitiveness and engage the employees." Top companies foster a culture where workers have a sense of belonging to the company and enjoy their job as an integral component of a full, rich life." -David Ballard

Other similarly well-meaning individuals in your lives offer another suggestion, furthering the confusion: "Follow your passion, and the money will come." This idea has been regularly reinforced by people who you see as symbols of achievement, including Steve Jobs. But can we really believe that pursuing your passion will always lead to financial success? The answer to this crucial issue might hold the secret to long-term satisfaction if you could establish with absolute certainty that passion and wealth go hand in hand.

"Happier employees are healthier and thus, in turn, keep the company in good health and great shape. Happy people reproduce like rabbits, so you must learn some great ways to promote better employee health."

Happiness has a multiplicative tendency; given enough time, it will spread throughout the entire organisation. More contented workers translate into more contented managers, and the cycle keeps on. It is easy for employees who like their jobs to become positive role models for their coworkers and inspire others to feel the same way. In addition to encouraging the employees under them to enjoy their work, happy managers are also less likely to act in a stereotypically authoritarian manner.

Happier workers encourage one another, which boosts productivity. While employees feel upbeat, they are more ready to help coworkers accomplish corporate objectives, especially when working on group assignments. Because many workers are embarrassed to ask for assistance when they need it, happy employees are also more inclined to ask for it when they need it. This is crucial for productivity.

A positive work atmosphere depends on contented employees. A motivated workforce has a good effect on the office atmosphere. Everyone is eager to go above and beyond the call of duty in this type of work atmosphere, making it perfect. Teams that are lighthearted, welcoming, and pleasant to work with deliver more effectively. Your staff won't be working just to earn their money at the end of the month if they are happy with the work they are doing. They will put more effort into achieving organisational goals and be more involved in the organisation's success. Each success of the company is celebrated by contented employees as their own. A content employee is simple to identify. You don't have to whine every day at work to be happy.

"A happy employee is someone who appreciates working with their team and looks forward to starting a new day of work each morning."

Given the trends in the workplace today, where employees are forgoing higher-paid positions in favour of ones that are more satisfying and likely to inspire them, keep in mind that contented customers are happy staff. It costs money to keep employees when you give them raises. The greatest benefit you can provide your employees is the potential to change the world via their work and to have a say in how the company develops.

Employee satisfaction is greatly influenced by benefits, including departmental and individual supervision, regular and clear communication about business events, and overall organisational direction. Employees who are at ease in their positions are motivated to perform well and frequently produce better outcomes.

Happy employees are proactive in both seeking and acting upon feedback. Use constructive criticism to encourage your staff to address problem areas and produce better results.In companies, ensuring employee satisfaction has become more and more important. Why? There is mounting evidence that successful businesses have content employees. According to one study, cheerful workers are up to 20% more productive than dissatisfied ones. Sales are increased by 37% when salespeople are happy, which is an even higher effect. The advantages don't stop there, either.

"Employee happiness is not a luxury, even in hard times; contented workers are inventive, creative, and dependable."

Managers and team leaders are aware that contented employees are productive employees. Why? Because happy employees are more motivated to work harder. People who are passionate about what they do will work far harder than others who are just doing it to get by. They will typically focus more intently on their job, ask for input when something isn't working, and be open to hearing opposing viewpoints. Employees who are content serve their clients or customers more effectively, get along with peers, juniors, and seniors, and improve the health of their firm as a whole. If you're a manager, you should make an effort to keep your staff content. They will be more productive and find their work more enjoyable as a result. Remember that for employees to grow professionally and reach their full potential, they require constructive criticism as well.

For any company to survive and operate well, having a content staff is crucial. Employees that are happier work harder, collaborate better in teams, and are overall more productive. However, why does pleasure boost productivity? Why does increased productivity usually result from a happier work environment? To be truly happy at work, you must adore both your job and your workplace. Unfortunately, for the majority of people, this is only a pipe dream. Many of us wake up dreading every single work day and practically have to drug yourselves with coffee all day long to get through it. Let's face it: even though you spend half of your waking hours at work, disliking your jobs (and typically the people that come with them too, such as bosses, clients, and coworkers) is a common theme in your pop culture, appearing in everything from movies to songs to everyday jokes. Organisations need to attract and retain individuals who like their professions since they are often highly competent at them. In addition to increasing an organisation's efficiency, content employees also help it attract the greatest talent available. On the other hand, when employees are dissatisfied, they make the barest of efforts to prevent being let go, at best, and at worst, they may utterly undermine the business.

"A productive, happy employee experience has emerged as the new contract between company and employee."
-Deloitte's 2017 Global Human Capital Trends report.

When considering a new job or promotion, the dilemma of choosing between a salary and passion doesn't simply affect those who are just entering the workforce. Research does indicate that living your passion leads to happiness, and that the combination of passion and happiness can lead to greater financial success, even if you can never completely disregard the desire to make money. Lack of enthusiasm for your work might be costly. Even if choosing to pursue a job centred on your passion won't make you suddenly wealthy, it will provide you with fulfilment and happiness in your work. Not everyone has an instinctive understanding of how crucial this is to living a happy life and, thus, how seriously negatively your happiness may be affected by not enjoying your job.

"Follow your passion, and the money will come."-Steve Jobs.

Values in an organisation are significant. And every organisation wants its employees to uphold these principles. But you frequently only acknowledge people based on their success at work. This frequently, but not always, coincides with upholding corporate ideals. Create a recognition program that also recognises individuals for upholding your key principles. Additionally, you'll generate additional chances for others to notice you in public.

Most businesses have a system in place for collecting employee input, such as a suggestion box or an open door policy. During performance reviews, the majority of managers want comments. However, because their criticism is never followed up on, employees frequently feel as though they are speaking into thin air. Additionally, it might be challenging for workers to understand how the business is reacting to employee feedback. That's a feedback loop that's not complete. By sending out brief "you asked, we listened" organisations that demonstrate how they are resolving employee complaints, HR teams and managers may close the feedback loop. The organisation's listening will be evident to its workers. Additionally, you'll foster better responsibility because they'll be aware of how the organisation plans to address problems. If team members believe the organisation is not keeping its commitments, they can provide further feedback.

What exactly constitutes employee wellbeing?

Ensuring employee wellbeing is much more than just providing a comfortable workplace with all the modern conveniences of the pre-pandemic era; it is an evolutionary revolution in and of itself. These days, the topic most in demand is wellness or well-being. Since the COVID-19 epidemic, organisations all around the world have realised how important it is to give priority to employee welfare.

Feeling wholesome, content, and socially connected are the foundations of wellbeing. It entails possessing the following qualities: excellent mental health and emotional stability; a sense of meaning or purpose; high levels of resilience; and the capacity to cope with stress. Wellness, in my opinion, is a constant process that calls for deliberate and persistent attention. For this reason, a lot of progressive wellness initiatives are moving toward a much more holistic strategy that incorporates not just the conventional physical wellbeing individuals typically identify with good health but also emotional, vocational, social, and intellectual components.

Given that so many individuals now work full-or part-time from home, maintaining a comprehensive view of overall wellness and satisfaction is becoming more and more crucial. The typical employee works about 50 hours each week and consumes around one-third of their meals there. Organisations must adopt a more comprehensive perspective on their employees' wellness if they want to change the culture of the organisation and make it more meaningful. There are five aspects of wellness that together constitute your whole well-being: physical, mental, social, intellectual, and spiritual wellbeing.

There are benefits to employee wellbeing beyond offering a wholesome food bar, a recreation area, or a gym at work. It involves giving workers plenty of opportunities to develop and maintain a comprehensive perspective on their wellness. Many individuals struggle to get through each day while living in a perpetual state of tension and worry. It's growing more and harder to go through each day without losing one's temper, whether it's due to relationships, parenting, job obligations, commuting in traffic, or, in most situations, a mix of some or all of these. For this reason, a lot of progressive wellness initiatives are moving toward a much more holistic strategy that incorporates not just the conventional physical wellbeing individuals typically identify with good health but also emotional, vocational, social, and intellectual components. Given that so many individuals now work full-or part-time from home, maintaining a comprehensive view of overall wellness and satisfaction is becoming more and more crucial.

Effective workplace wellness programs boost employees' loyalty, improve work performance, raise productivity, and lower attrition rates, according to a poll conducted by ASSOCHAM (Associated Chambers of Commerce and Industry of India). Workplace wellness basically refers to a health campaign that a company adopts as a policy to encourage healthy behaviors and to enhance the general well-being of the employees. The workplace wellness program enhances employees' physical, mental, emotional, vocational, and social well-being. All the elements that a person needs to live their personal and professional lives are included in holistic wellbeing.

Living a greater quality of life obviously requires maintaining your ideal level of wellbeing. Wellness is important because everything a person does and feels has a direct impact on how well they are feeling and how well they are achieving their professional goals. This has an impact on how well the organisation performs. Organisations may gain a lot by holding frequent wellness seminars and wellness transformation sessions since it shows employees that you care about their health and wellbeing, which boosts morale and performance.

While an organisation can give its employees a wide range of activities as part of a wellness program, some of the activities that can improve workers' emotional, social, and mental health include: being attentive involves paying attention to both what is going on inside of you and outside of you without passing judgement. It aids in increasing mental awareness and fostering a closer relationship with oneself. As a result, it helps the organisation boost efficiency while creating a hardy and contented staff. Mindfulness has already been incorporated into the cultures of companies like Google, Nike, and Apple.Among the practices of mindfulness are:

- Mindful Meditation: This type of meditation, which focuses on breathing, helps to bring the mind into the present moment and keeps it from daydreaming or worrying.
- Mindful Gratitude: Being grateful and kind to coworkers and others in general is a fantastic way to enjoy cooperation and collaboration. When compared to those who don't, people who show thankfulness are happier, healthier, and nearly 50% more productive.
- Mindful Affirmation: Personal affirmations encourage optimism and serve as a gentle reminder to practice mindfulness.

According to a 2020 Gallup poll of American workers, the majority of Americans either put in their time without showing any love or drive for their profession or dread going to work every day. Businesses should avoid this. Disengaged workers cost companies money, as is widely known (measuring into the billions annually). The benefits are similarly substantial.

How to bring positive work culture that makes employees more productive?

Genuinely happy team members will encourage one another and contribute to the development of a compassionate and respected workplace culture. Respect and empathy enable you to comprehend another person's feelings, their struggles, and how to show them respect. This will improve the work ethic of your team and facilitate the development of better relationships with your staff.

For decades, you have been told that employee engagement is a crucial component of a successful organisation. It measures how passionately workers feel about their work. Their level of dedication to the company is what matters. It's the extra effort they put into their jobs. The key is psychological control.

This is not simply feel-good material. High levels of employee engagement and well-being are strongly correlated with profitability, decreased turnover, customer loyalty, and many other company outcomes. For more than 80 years, the Gallup organisation has gathered information on employee engagement in 160 nations. The typical level of involvement among Gallup's American clientele is around 35%. This demonstrates that around two thirds of the employees polled are not completely engaged in their work. Disengaged workers alone cost the American economy $400 billion in lost productivity each year.

"Engagement at work is positive. Being happy is much better."

A happy workplace leads to a happy business. You will change titles, arrange a good parking spot, offer a group lunch, and publicly honor achievements inside the office. You'll also support employees' personal growth and development, whether they choose to do so by accepting challenges or new roles, enrolling in classes to build new skills, or learning more about the firm by going on official business trips. Having a positive attitude while entering the office as the boss and making sure that everyone feels important are two things that cannot be overstated.

Customers like speaking with positive personnel because they are more likely to pay attention and provide better service. Customer satisfaction rises following favourable encounters with your personnel, which may boost customer retention and business profitability. According to the Social Market Foundation's happiness survey, unhappy workers often produce less work than happy ones.When it came time to work, the group that had been given snacks and 10 minutes to view comedic films was not only more engaged than the control group, but it was also 12% more productive. Joy spreads and influences the team's overall energy. A positive corporate culture multiplies the beneficial effects across the whole organisation. This increases teamwork among your employees and increases overall employee engagement.

In my experience, workers seldom get dissatisfied or quit because of money. When they do lose interest, it is typically because they dislike their supervisor, feel unengaged, or believe they have reached the end of their educational journey. Positive workplace cultures and environments are very helpful because they promote cooperation and communication, which raises engagement and presents an opportunity for coworkers to learn from one another. Additionally, you occasionally recognise employees at all levels of the company for outstanding performance or exceptional effort.

It's already too late to try to keep a worker by giving him or her a raise. Early on, screen candidates for fit and provide chances for advancement to reflect that value. Find employees that share the operational values of your organisation. You are passionate about entrepreneurship and making a positive difference. Following a positive effort, our team members are often rewarded with higher-value projects. These compliments are free but offer valuable public acknowledgement for a job well done, essentially paying individuals in the form of highly prized social currency.

The frequency of rewards matters more than their magnitude. According to business research, consumers will be happier for longer when they receive smaller, more frequent compliments and prizes rather than a single, big, occasional pleasant event. The majority of workers respond better to little dosages given every few days rather than the greatest rewards or increases, which "burn off" in less than a year.

By helping workers in other aspects of their lives, employers may increase their pay in a variety of ways. To preserve employees' earnings, you might extend your life or disability insurance coverage. Employees are pleased with other auxiliary benefits, including dental, vision, and wellness. Additionally, effective rewards to keep staff workers happy and healthy are gym memberships and metro passes. Higher benefits are necessary to show your workers that you genuinely care about them and their families.

Gains in productivity and profitability for businesses with high employee engagement are proportionally considerable (workers who are happy and fulfilled in their roles). Clearly, an organisation's success depends on its employees' enthusiasm. So, how do passion and engagement affect your life, finances, and future? The most obvious thing to note is how much time we really spend working, not to mention how demoralising it is to waste even more valuable time hating your workdays. Approximately 90,000 hours, or more than 10 years of your life, will be spent working if your career lasts 40 years.

That's a lot of time to spend on something you don't find enjoyable. However, if your task makes you feel "flown" and is satisfying enough for you to enjoy it, it may not even seem like work.

Above all other emotions, love is the most wonderful sensation there is. But when you genuinely care about someone, you want nothing more than to see them happy and fortunate, whether or not you are around. The desire to provide them with all the happiness and comfort in the world spurs you on to work more and generate more income to meet their demands.

On the other hand, we require a salary in order to support our families and ourselves in this world. There is nothing wrong with wanting to make money; the issue starts when this desire oversteps all limits and becomes an obsession. As they are essential to every person, don't allow money to take over your life; instead, strike a balance between the two. The money will come if you love what you do and give it your all. You have a lot higher chance of finding satisfaction as a result of this, which gives you a sense of real purpose.

"Do what you love, and you'll never have to work a day in your life, is a proverb that you've probably heard. Don't make money your main priority. Instead, go after your passions and master them to the point that others can't stop staring at you. You will be more than prepared to give your job your all when you see it as an integral part of your life rather than something apart from it. That desire will make you stand out and provide opportunities for potential career advancement."

Trust is the key to happy, devoted workers. For both employees and employers, trust is a strong basis on which to create a connection that is meaningful, instructive, and mutually profitable. The key to having contented and devoted workers is completely obvious. Many things have been said and written about how to keep your staff satisfied and devoted, but recent American research claims that all it takes is trust. The study demonstrates the different dimensions of workplace trust and how it relates to other job-related characteristics.

American research team polled 54,827 individuals between June and September of last year. Compared to 26% of those who can't do anything without being informed beforehand, 72% of employees who can act and make decisions (or feel trusted) are content with their jobs. 76% of respondents whose bosses had little faith in them planned to look for a new job, compared to 54% of those whose bosses trusted them. Individuals earning more when they are having complete faith in their managers, compared to only 63% of those earning less than. In comparison to 59% of those with less than two years of experience, 76% of those with more than ten years of experience reported that their bosses trust them. The study's findings confirm the value of having faith in your workers. It demonstrates that employees who are trusted more are likely to produce better jobs and be more devoted. Additionally, it demonstrates how race, employment experience, and even income level are all related to trust.

Finding a job that makes you feel fulfilled and in flow might have benefits for your career trajectory that you can't even begin to imagine. You would agree that happiness and success are strongly correlated, but I also point out that happiness typically comes before success. This might be taken to suggest that being happy in your job sets the tone for your career and aids in your rapid advancement.

You may be on the path to future success—and possibly a higher salary than you had anticipated for yourself—if you are working in a lower-paying position but are enthusiastic about what you do and are giving it your best. A different perspective on the connection between wealth and happiness is that, while some financial stability does provide people a certain amount of comfort and pleasure, the amount of satisfaction that can be obtained from wealth is strictly limited. People who made substantially more money experienced less stress in their lives and reported feeling generally pleased. This might be a crucial issue to bring up if someone in your life pushes you to pursue a career as a doctor or lawyer rather than one for which you have a passion.

Some of you may need to spend some time on the job before discovering your interests and abilities, because you don't all know them right away. There are a few things you can do if you find yourself at a crossroads to make sure you choose the best course of action for that point in your life. It's difficult to know exactly what your passion is at a young age since, it can grow and even alter over time. Therefore, it may be advantageous to consider your whole "purpose" rather than just your "passion" when determining what to do next.

Does the organisation you're thinking about joining share your goals?

What does your intuition have to say about your true calling? Your workdays may seem shorter and provide you with an opportunity for growth if you spend them doing something you care about with people who share those feelings. In other words, the time you spend working to get that salary will be beneficial on deeper levels.

According to me, life is not a straight path. You commonly make the error of believing that establishing a career entails beginning at the bottom of one ladder and climbing it steadily to the top. However, in practice, it is not how most people's journeys really pan out. Opportunities never come your way in advance, and you can never know what will happen if you accept them (or don't take them).

"Living a happy life means taking the time to identify your strengths and hobbies, embracing them, and coming up with your own personal definition of happiness."

Ideally, you will discover that you can eventually make money from your interests, so that you may combine the best of both worlds. In a recent white paper, research on the elements that influence employee and company satisfaction was conducted. More than 12,000 workers in the United States and Canada responded to the poll, which is based on their responses. The paper investigated key factors that influence employee happiness and provided insightful insights into what makes for an enjoyable and productive work environment for employees. This raises the question of how businesses might increase employee contentment.

It is an emotive term that employees use to describe the quality of experiences at work, or more specifically, how they feel and how well they are doing. Various groups of individuals have different definitions of what "happiness at work" is. In 2020, managers discovered the hard way that you can't simply turn a switch and alter the way a firm is managed. You must maintain readiness with office technology that can support a variety of evolving work styles. A company that promotes workplace wellness, issued their yearly Workplace Health Report. The conclusions drawn from this study make it very evident that workers are still coping with high levels of stress and anxiety at work.

Since the coronavirus epidemic, there have been significant changes in the well-being culture in many businesses, including the elimination of long commutes and more employee flexibility. But as we all know, change rarely occurs quickly. Additionally, there won't always be a major catastrophe on the world stage to spur action. Since the epidemic, allowing individuals the freedom to adapt their jobs around their hectic lives has had a significant positive influence on wellbeing. Through multiple research, it has been discovered several intriguing patterns about how to foster an environment where workers are encouraged to enjoy their work, leading to the production of more meaningful and thoughtful work.

Positive attitudes in the workplace are extremely beneficial to you and your team. Here are few justifications for why you should make an attempt to raise staff morale at your company. When people are not paralysed by fear and worry, they make better judgments. Compared to stressed-out employees, who frequently become distracted, those with good employee morale take calculated risks. The confidence you, as the employer, build in your employees via respect and gratitude plays a part in inspiring this clarity and conduct. Unhappy employees are more inclined to look for new employment. Employee retention is negatively impacted by an unfavourable work environment. As a result, there will inevitably be staff turnover, which puts further strain on your company because you will need to spend time and resources conducting interviews with potential replacements. According to Adobe's State of Creativity survey, happy employees are more creative, which is very advantageous for the expansion of your company.

Here are those important steps you can take right away to help your company find qualified job candidates. First, make the organisation seem like a fun place to work to attract potential employees. How does your employment page appear? What kind of interest is it drawing? Top prospects: are they enthusiastic about your business? Are they interested in your job openings because your branding suggests a fun place to work? I've already examined hundreds of job pages, and most of them are at best dull. Your job description must be captivating and intriguing. Talk about the possibility of professional progression, offer video testimonials from current workers, display a day in the life film, and tell tales about performing an excellent job. Now, a fantastic company's employment page extends an invitation. Looking over these sites, people who are bored with their existing occupations hear themselves saying, "I'd really want to work there."

How to create a positive employee onboarding experience?

Setting up your newly hired employees and your organisation for success requires a successful onboarding process. An efficient onboarding process for new hires encourages engagement, shortens the learning curve, lowers the likelihood of attrition, and develops your future leaders.

"Your most valuable resource is people. And making the finest first impression possible will boost everyone's return on investment."

And the proper way to do this is by developing worthwhile job offers, making plans for career succession, and giving new recruits the necessary tools. But there is something that is more important. Employee onboarding is that thing. It will determine an employee's career path in your company from the first day (and before). When a positive onboarding process is effective, it gives new employees the chance to develop into the most effective brand ambassadors.

The process of onboarding must be remote because remote working has become the norm for most organisations. The golden rule is still "Remote or Not," even when technology or the preparedness for remote onboarding might operate as a differentiator in the efficiency and efficacy of the process. The transformation of an external applicant into an employee is known as the onboarding process in layman's terms. There are many ways to succeed in this process, but it's important to realise that the fundamentals apply to all of the onboarding tools.

"You must succeed at work before you can succeed in the marketplace."

The first impression a new employee will have of your company is based on the employee onboarding process. Giving them all the resources and knowledge they require to become fully engaged in their new position and your business is crucial if you want it to be a long-lasting relationship. Apple established the iBuddy concept in order to pair new workers with people who have a thorough understanding of the Apple culture. Here, new employees are partnered with a veteran worker who is not on their core team so they may ask questions about their job, the business, the culture, or a particular work practise. iBuddies are still relevant today, 30 years after the system's debut, and many other businesses, including Microsoft, have embraced them.

According to the Harvard Business Review, organisations with standardised onboarding procedures see a 50% improvement in retention. Given that the average cost-per-hire in the US is $4,4252, you should make every effort to retain the talent you have already invested in.

When a new employee joins the company, they have access to Vodafone's app, which walks them through their onboarding process. The app is designed to make the onboarding process more convenient by allowing new hires to fill out their requirements. Vodafone, a telecom giant with employees all over the world, understands the importance of a great onboarding experience. While other companies have complex frameworks and documentation, Vodafone created its own employee onboarding application.

However, shockingly few businesses give the onboarding process the attention and resources it deserves. That may be the case because too many organisations prioritise procedures and paper work during onboarding, failing to give adequate consideration to a comprehensive, people-centered approach for developing and keeping talent.

Google's onboarding is an inspiration to many businesses since it focuses on the managers at the other end of the hiring process, in contrast to the examples above, who are known for their entertaining office activities and excellent benefits packages. A new hire's managers receive an automated notification 24 hours prior to their start date with 5 specific instructions: assigning them a peer or buddy; discussing their role and responsibilities; assisting them in getting to know their coworkers; setting up employee check-ins for the first six months; and encouraging them to be open about potential issues.Since the manager is carrying the bulk of the onboarding, the new hire gains more first-hand knowledge of their role and responsibilities. This is a great example of an onboarding process that is designed with human behaviour and experience in mind. The goal in this case is to have a short time frame between the email and the new hire's starting date, so the tasks stay fresh in their minds.

Due to research showing that effective onboarding may increase employee retention by 82%, onboarding is crucial. However, it has been shown that 22% of businesses don't have an official onboarding program. Additionally, it was shown that just 13% of employees strongly think that their company onboards new employees well. It is important to note that despite the fact that onboarding has been shown to be an excellent strategy for employee retention, it is often done improperly.

"Your company's greatest asset is its employees, therefore it's critical that you pay special attention to the hiring and onboarding processes."

Business success depends on finding the appropriate people and assisting them in reaching their full potential. Whether the mentoring relationship lasts 90 days or a year, both the mentor and the supervisor should plan regular check-ins and meetings to see if the new hire has any questions, offer continuous feedback, and reduce the likelihood that the new hire will feel alone.

Take the new recruit out to lunch with one or more departmental members. If the job is distant, consider setting up a casual zoom lunch and asking attendees to consider how they might make the new recruit feel at home. Make sure the new employee is familiar with the company's core business, departmental culture, and the background of the position they have been hired to fill. This may be done through a series of meetings with all pertinent coworkers and managers.

What HR should create a fresh personnel file and any other necessary files. Prepare a special welcome message or video from management and coworkers to present to the new recruit. Plan important tasks for new hires to complete during their first week on the job so they feel wanted and occupied. Inform coworkers about the upcoming arrival of new hires. Get everything ready for remote work or mail it, and have the new recruit sign a document about business property or equipment. You might need to be a little more proactive when managing a remote workforce. For instance, make sure the business laptop comes the Friday before the start date on Monday so that your employee is prepared on day one. Assign a departmental onboarding mentor who may introduce the new hire to the company's and the department's practises in a less formal manner. A CNBC study on workplace happiness found that 57% of employees who have mentors are extremely pleased with their employment, bringing the overall satisfaction rate to 91%. Compare that to the more than 4 in 10 unmentored employees who claim to have thought about leaving their job in the previous three months. Especially if the job will be done remotely, make explicit your company's expectations for significant workplace rituals, which include goals for productivity.

Whether online or in person, welcoming a new employee is just as vital as welcoming a new client. Have your new hire's coworker or supervisor assist them in completing all pertinent and necessary documentation; discuss any pertinent administrative processes, performance objectives, and remuneration. Some businesses halt the onboarding process after the first week, but this can make new workers feel lost and alone at work. However, best practises suggest that in order to provide new recruits the assistance they need to be effective, employee onboarding programmes should run for at least 90 days.

What would be your strategic approaches to make an engaged workplace?

There isn't a single method that can guarantee your workplace will become more engaged. What works for the business next door won't always work for your business.

- Create activities and programs that are exclusive to your brand and that can easily be tied back into your business culture, since one of the key components of employee happiness is the sense of belonging that employees have toward the company as a whole. And don't be scared to try something new when it comes to how you interact with your employees.
- Learn from the outcomes of your prior projects to better focus your employee happiness efforts in the future. Employee happiness is a continuous activity.
- Start out Fridays in the summer or winter with team hybrid happy hours. Reserve the final half hour of each shorter Friday for your remote and hybrid teams to gather one more time for the week with a beverage of choice in their hands before letting everyone go to enjoy their weekend early. These collective wind-down sessions are an excellent chance for remote and hybrid teams made up of members who have never met in person to bond in a less formal context than a usual work gathering.
- Connectivity is the key to fostering employee happiness, and using packaged events to bring everyone together while they are still geographically separated is one method to promote connection for scattered staff.

- Create group projects that encourage team members to get out and be active so they can later discuss their experiences with one another. Organisations may demonstrate to staff how much they appreciate their health and fitness by implementing movement programs that get them away from their desks and into the open air.
- Which comes first, workers' happiness or their sense of happiness at work? Employee happiness and happiness actually go hand in hand. Without the other, there would be a lacklustre workplace and disengaged workers. When you don't understand the benefits of face-to-face happiness, it can be difficult to keep remote staff motivated and engaged.
- For remote team managers, employee happiness and happiness are their top priorities. This issue affects both firms with blended teams and those where everyone works remotely (both in-office and remote employees). The good news is that remote employees are eager and happy to contribute to the team and come up with fresh ideas to improve the corporate culture. They are just as invested in the vision, objectives, and expansion of the business as everyone else. It is the responsibility of remote team managers to be aware of the distinct difficulties posed by working remotely and to actively try to reduce conflict for their staff.

How to handle disengaged employees?

Actively disengaged workers are extremely unsettling. They wish to transmit their negativity to other employees since they are not only unhappy and unproductive but also dissatisfied. They can also do far worse, as I can tell you from my experience as an employment lawyer.

Approximately 13% of workers, according to Gallup, are actively disengaged. As a manager, you must be very clear that those who are actively disengaged must either try to change now or face expulsion from your organisation. A sustained effort at recovery is just not worthwhile. Actively disengaged employees are a dangerous and harmful factor that has to be eliminated.

Let me explain to you how to determine if you employ any of these individuals and what to do in that case. Start by posing this query to yourself. Is there anyone currently employed by your organisation whose departure would make you feel more relieved than angry? If the response is indeed, you must further investigate the matter.

Do they generally have a disengaged attitude or are circumstances to blame?

Even employees who have a typically upbeat outlook might lose engagement owing to external factors such as a truly unpleasant supervisor or no salary increases for three years. Make sure there isn't a valid explanation for that disengagement, and if there is, accept responsibility for it and work to address it. The next step is to let them know that their behaviour is undesirable and won't be permitted if you find out that it has less to do with the circumstances than with their overall attitude. Call them out on it by issuing a written or verbal warning. Most businesses have a policy requiring this. It would be wise to approach this conversation like a coach would. Make it clear that while you'll do everything you can to address the situation, they also have a duty to change their overall mindset.

Therefore, it's crucial that you check to see if there isn't a valid explanation for that disengagement and, if there is, accept it and work to address it. The next step is to inform them that their behaviour is undesirable and will not be permitted if you see that their disengagement is less related to the circumstances than it is to their overall attitude. Call them out on it by issuing a warning in writing or verbally. In most businesses, this is a rule that must be followed. Approaching this conversation as a coach might be a smart idea. Make it obvious that you'll do all you can to address the situation, but that they also bear some of the responsibility for changing their overall attitude. And they'll have to consider the idea if things don't start getting better right now. And they risk being disciplined or fired if things don't start getting better right away. Remember, let them take responsibility if it is their issue. Now, adhere to these general guidelines while coaching an employee. Criticise in private, be precise, criticise the behaviour rather than the person, offer helpful guidance, and keep detailed records of everything.

Finally, involve HR in the serious situations. It's typically a good idea, even if policy does not demand it. HR can offer a neutral assessment of the circumstance and perhaps offer some helpful advice on how to address it. They'll also work to ensure that you abide by the rules and regulations of the business. Employees that are actively disengaged pose a serious danger to a business. They can exhaust you and lead to serious issues. Do what you can to assist them in succeeding and changing their behaviour. Give them a chance to succeed. It's time for them to go on, though, if they are unwilling to adapt.

A U.K. study found that 33% of the participants would genuinely accept a wage reduction in exchange for the ability to continue working remotely and with more flexibility. It could be worthwhile to ask your staff how they feel about returning to the office (if that was your objective) now that limitations have been loosened even more. If you've made a permanent commitment to working from home, you might want to consider this the other way around. It's possible that some team members are experiencing the negative consequences of working remotely. Here are a few strategies you can use to start giving your employees' happiness a higher priority and, as a result, produce a more engaged workforce in your company.

"Our people-first approach, which has guided our company since it was founded, means when our company does well, our people do really, really well. Our people work incredibly hard and deserve to share in Southwest's success." -Gary Kelly, CEO, Southwest Airlines

According to one's experience, the new employee's acceptance is what matters most in order to provide them with that "WOW" moment, also known as customer delight. Always keep the organisation's long-term view in mind.

How to create "WOW" moments for your employees?

The following considerations must be made whether working remotely or in person: meticulous planning of the entire procedure is essential. This will make it easier to identify even the smallest obstacles and devise a strategy to get rid of them. Plan out every aspect of the program beginning on Day 0.

- Identify the stakeholders.
- Prepare to define expectations.
- Learn a little more about the applicant before hiring them.
- Do something to create that personal touch.
- Help foster a cultural fit.

For instance, picking up the employee from their home, as was done on the first day, Onboarding should take place over a longer period of time. Avoid trying to overwhelm the person with too much information in a short amount of time. Whenever feasible, use technology. To aid their learning while they are on the road, you may leverage social media platforms, develop applications, or build online training courses. The list goes on and on.

Keep your relationship with them going. Once a person joins an organisation, their responsibilities do not end there. It must be made sure that they are aware that a hearing aid is there for them when they feel lost or disengaged, in addition to having fun and participating in the many planned activities.

Buddy programs inside the organisation are also effective at helping new hires adjust to their new environment. Let them enjoy themselves while going through these processes as you succeed in these areas. They will be better able to connect with the other new hires, the team, HR, etc. thanks to this.

"When the onboarding process is successful, it gives us the chance to transform these new hires into our most effective brand ambassadors."

Recent Gallup study findings support that businesses with content and motivated staff are 21% more successful than those with a less motivated workforce. Additionally, these businesses exhibit stronger customer interactions, fewer workplace mishaps, and fewer sick days. In this chapter, I'll try to delve into the strategies for fostering a productive workplace where employees may advance their careers and contribute to the business.

According to 83% of American companies, a lack of skilled labour has an effect on their earnings and potential expansion. The skill disparity affects both sides equally. Employees are also affected by talent shortages, so it's not just businesses that suffer. The workforce's inability to compete with peers and follow the desired care route is caused by the skills mismatch. Employees should review their competence every two to three years as a workaround and keep an eye on labour market developments to be the first to adopt new skills.

Employers must help their employees close the skill gaps. They must first list the precise hard and soft abilities needed for the targeted profession or function. The implementation of future-proofing against potential talent market developments is crucial next. Using information about the existing skills gap and future skill needs, organisation can provide skill-targeted internal programs, cultivate future leaders, and upskill the workforce. With all these initiatives in place, staff members can clearly see the future talents they'll need to acquire in order to remain competitive within and outside of the organisation's talent market.

Think about varying the tasks your team members perform by giving them additional responsibilities or developing their work positions. You'll be able to by using stretch assignments:

- Encourage your employees to adapt to a new role by encouraging them to leave their comfort zone.
- Develop an employee with a mindset that is business-focused (new challenges and responsibilities boost employee happiness and leadership).
- Educate and train your employees. This increases staff happiness and work satisfaction.

Leadership development is prioritised by 58% of businesses. To increase employee happiness in 2022 and going ahead, businesses will concentrate on improving their middle management suite and emotional intelligence. Foster leadership among middle-and junior-level managers as opposed to concentrating on the C-suite and staff members who have been with the organisation for three years or more. Managers may improve team morale and establish rapport by incorporating coaching techniques.

People in large organisation are frequently imprisoned in their silos and only know their immediate coworkers. HR may gain from skill management software to identify significant talents, possible mentors, and prospects for skill upskilling. The matching algorithm assists HR executives in gaining a bird's-eye perspective of talents and competences, connecting the workforce, opening up tasks and job responsibilities, and facilitating communication between HR and workers.

Recently, the learning paradigm changed from a "supervising" pattern to one that emphasises "collaboration" and "mentoring." It indicates that leading businesses have begun implementing a peer-to-peer learning strategy. Such a strategy encourages peer mentoring and training, not that of outside consultants or supervisors. Peer-to-peer learning offers a number of noteworthy benefits.

- When learning with others, people first feel less anxious about making mistakes or failing.
- Peer-to-Peer training supports greater decision-making, employee empowerment, and self-governance inside an organisation.

- It enables the expansion of information exchange and expertise inside a business.

A common feature of contemporary skill management platforms is the mentoring-matching feature, which encourages bottom-up learning and makes peer-to-peer learning more open, creative, and transparent. The matching system links workers, highlighting mentors who could be a good fit. This result in a distinctive and customised value proposition that is unique to each of the greatest value-creating jobs and builds on the overarching value proposition that is applicable to all talent in the organisation.

A common feature of contemporary skill management platforms is the mentoring-matching feature, which encourages bottom-up learning and makes peer-to-peer learning more open, creative, and transparent. The matching system links workers, highlighting mentors who could be a good fit. The workers can better help one another in certain projects or tasks by doing this.The mentorship programme JetBlue Scholars, run by the American airline JetBlue, is a striking illustration of peer-to-peer learning. In this programme, more experienced coworkers train and advise junior coworkers who lack a college degree. The firm was able to decrease tuition costs by around $2.8 million as a consequence, and employee happiness rose to an impressive 85%.

Again, an advantage of developing your top talent program is the ability to create situations like this one where the organisation and the person benefit equally. You've witnessed another advantage of the program for business as well as the best talent.

What if you built a database or talent pool of the people your software recognised as having talent?

Then, you kept track of any upcoming or current openings before they were announced. Members of my team really carried out this action. They then conducted a weekly evaluation of the available jobs and combed through your pool for prospective matches, many of which they found promptly. In reality, you would have a good success rate in connecting the right abilities with the right jobs. In addition to saving the business time in filling important roles and giving your best personnel a fresh opportunity to further their careers, we also made significant financial savings for the business.

An external headhunter will charge 20 to 30% of the executive's yearly salary for the privilege of placing an executive in an executive job. This may potentially save hundreds of thousands of dollars annually, but don't tell the headhunters since they won't like it. You now have it. You can now clearly see how your efforts in developing a top talent program have benefited the business as well as the top talents you have discovered. Determine your program's efficacy. You can never know how successful a project or program has been until you measure it. Accurate assessment is essential because it reveals the genuine effects of your top talent program, which may either support or undermine your business case for more initiatives. Measurement may be difficult because you have to make sure you're measuring the correct things in the appropriate ways. Consider it in this manner. You would compare your results before and after if you were a runner looking to determine if a new training plan was helping you improve your time, right?

Are you really measuring the proper things if you time how long it takes you to run a specific distance and compare it to running in the woods after on a track?

The most accurate method would be to time yourself as opposed to using a stopwatch to measure the same distance on the same surface. Most likely not. The efficiency of your program should also be taken into account, both now and in the future. As an illustration, when I ran training sessions to get people ready for my programs, I asked for real-time feedback so that I could modify and enhance them as I went. Based on the quick response from your consumers, this started a cycle of continual improvement. I also tracked other employees indicators over time, such as the retention rates of top talent in comparison to other workers who didn't have access to the same possibilities for professional growth.

I also examined the proportion of top performers who received promotions over one or two years compared to your whole population. I had outstanding results with one of the programs I ran. To be more specific, I was able to retain 90% of your best talent following a year-long development program, and 50% of that talent had moved into new or larger responsibilities.

Last but not least, evaluating concrete and intangible costs and benefits is one of the most difficult components of measuring people initiatives. Calculating the savings your firm experiences as a consequence of placing your best employees in critical roles versus what it would have cost to have an external headhunter fill those jobs is an example of a tangible advantage.

If you can estimate it, some less obvious advantages can include the amount of money your business saves by not having a crucial job open for a prolonged length of time or the degree of engagement your top talent and workers in general experience as a result of operating a top talent program. Prior to the commencement of your program, it's critical to consider what you can assess and the most effective ways to do so.

As you progress through the curriculum and learn more, you will probably modify or add to these precautions. After the program is finished, it would be wonderful to meet with the talent and executives of your firm to discuss it and integrate their suggestions into the next edition. Okay, excellent! You now know how to gauge the success of your top talent program and show how important it is to the organisation from both a business and human resources standpoint.

You might believe that you can relax and catch your breath now that you've designed and managed your first top talent program. It doesn't stop here, so don't relax for too long. People and organisations are both continually undergoing change. Nothing ever remains static. It's possible that the folks who were your talents last year won't continue to be them the following year.

"Employees are driven to get more active in the organisation and are proven to create higher-quality work when they are proud of where they work and are in line with the organisation's vision and goals."

The business plan may change from one year to the next, necessitating the hiring of new executives with diverse skill sets. The future may be anticipated and prepared for, but very few people are consistently accurate forecasters. If you're interested in learning more about culture transformation, you can find my culture change course on LinkedIn. Every one to three years, the majority of firms will run versions of their top talent initiatives. For the reasons listed below, I suggest every two years.

As you may have found, developing and successfully implementing a top talent program requires a lot of time, resources, and money. Most of the time, running your nomination and selection processes will take you several months, and running the development phase will take you a full year. It will also demand a major time and energy commitment from you, your team, the leadership team, the communications department, and the management of your business.

- Employee pride in their organisation is the main factor influencing satisfaction at work.
- Another element that enhances employee satisfaction in several ways is giving employees the freedom to make decisions on their own or with little guidance. According to 26% of respondents, they have little to no opportunity for creative expression, and 23% believe they have little to no influence over their job.
- Behavioural change must start at the top for there to be a positive, inspiring business culture. The purpose of work is collaboration. For scattered teams, this is especially true.
- Connecting with coworkers is important for employee happiness and may even be a more powerful motivator than other factors. In fact, it is discovered that the main source of job satisfaction for workers returning to the workplace is their coworkers, cited by 54% of respondents.
- The interactions among coworkers are what make work fun, and they are essential to building a team that looks forward to going to work every day. Even if your organisation isn't quite ready to go back into offices,

making connections on both a personal and professional level needs to be a top concern.

- Happiness at work has been shown to increase team members' productivity by about 13% while also enhancing their general well-being.
- You may accomplish workplace happiness by inviting a speaker to spark fresh discussions, scheduling regular virtual get-togethers for new team members, or planning team off-site activities.
- In order for employees to identify the communication style that works best for them, connection points should occur both company-wide and one-on-one. These chances might signify more than you think, inspiring fresh concepts, creating bonds with team members, and offering brainstorming spaces.
- In the long run, these chances can also result in relationships that allow for peer advice and cooperation and foster a feeling of community for each team member.
- A critical component of any successful organisational culture is the ability to offer both constructive and positive feedback.
- Being surrounded by individuals who share your opinions is not beneficial for anyone's development or progress. On the other hand, being unrelentingly critical can simply demoralise your employees.
- Finding the right balance when providing feedback that is both supportive and constructive is crucial.
- This brings to mind the concept of open communication throughout your business. It's never a good idea to make assumptions about what will work for your team. There must be two-way communication so that you may ultimately achieve a workable arrangement.

- A culture of constructive, open communication will be supported by setting up an environment where teams feel comfortable offering and receiving feedback on a frequent basis.
- Open communication results in a workforce that can carry out their duties efficiently and productively without being afraid to engage in difficult conversations.
- Communication in the workplace may be challenging. The issues are further compounded by hybrid work since so much of the non-verbal communication that facilitates discussion is lost.
- Conversations about essential issues like duties, feedback, and workload are undoubtedly more crucial now, but they can be difficult to start, especially over Zoom.
- There has been a need for more open dialogue at work during the previous year. According to a recent SHRM poll, 59% of Americans who reported that workplace culture has genuinely improved since the pandemic's start attribute this improvement to communication.
- A lack of openness and communication at the top frequently causes this confusion. For managers, the past two years have ushered in a new era that has necessitated the adoption of an entirely new skill set.
- Managers now must be transparent and accountable in their leadership. Managers now must be transparent and accountable in their leadership. These new abilities must become the norm if businesses want to keep fostering work environments where people can flourish.
- You might consider what will inspire your team as you sit and think. However, asking is sometimes the wisest course of action. What may motivate them? Why do

they do it? What do they hold dear? There might be ten alternative responses.

- However, you may then discuss the best compromise with your management team. It's hard to satisfy everyone all the time, but you should always strive to consider other viewpoints.
- Having a contemporary, exciting workspace may have a significant influence on employee satisfaction, regardless of whether your employees are working from home more frequently, returning to a more hybrid working style, or embracing other new working practices.
- Both big and small businesses are using tech tools to promote their cultures. One Workplace, for instance, leverages our technology to provide an engaging experience across the board. This investment in cutting-edge infrastructure may boost organisational pride by portraying the business as tech-savvy, adaptable, and focused on touchpoints for employee involvement.
- The study also discovered that employees might be encouraged to work more when their employers show signs that they are improving, supporting business objectives, or developing professionally.
- The use of a Smart Campus newsfeed to include employee highlights, promoting amazing work by team members or workplace triumphs, is one excellent way to leverage an employee experience.
- By centralising employee recognition into a seamless experience that is readily available to all workers, this encourages employee appreciation throughout the whole business.
- According to managers, employees should be given more chances to accept full responsibility and be given

the freedom to submit their own ideas.

- Scheduling meetings where staff members may share their ideas or brainstorm with a group of peers to generate new concepts, receive feedback, and participate in the creative process is one approach to doing this. This may be accomplished by cutting down on the time required for administrative duties like scheduling meetings.
- Employee freedom to work where they choose is a plus, as is making it simple to locate coworkers.
- It should go without saying that all employees deserve to be treated fairly and with respect. This was cited as another factor affecting worker pleasure.
- As teams continue to be dispersed throughout various remote work locations, it is essential to ensure that all employees have equal access to resources and information. This is especially true as teams continue to be spread across diverse, remote work sites.
- Everyone, from new hires to C-level executives to entry-level employees, can use and benefit from workplace experience technology, such as our Smart Campus solution.
- Work-life balance is crucial, and utilising technology may help hybrid and remote workers feel just as connected as those who work in an office setting. Whether on a real campus or a virtual one, all employees may enjoy the same experience thanks to our Smart Campus software.
- You may save time and tension by consolidating employee experiences into a single mobile app rather than having them switch between many tools and procedures at work. Nearly 2.5 times as many workers are pleased as those who believe their employment is

"simply work" when they feel their work is worthwhile.

- To ensure that the company's vision and the responsibilities people play in attaining it are received, it is essential to communicate objectives and successes, especially at big businesses.

- It has been discovered that workplace camaraderie enhances employee collaboration, cooperation, and communication. Employees who get along well with people on their team are 2.5 times more likely to be satisfied with their jobs than those who do not.

- By encouraging networking, understanding where to locate people, and working close to teams that will help you be most productive, it is crucial to maintain those ties with colleagues when employees come and go through a flexible work model.

- Believe that a single app may enable employees to take charge of their workdays and workspaces, feel valued by the company, concentrate on meaningful work, encourage work-life balance, foster strong workplace relationships, and foster a feeling of corporate pride.

- When it comes to employee happiness, it's important to keep workers motivated and productive, whether they're working onsite or remotely. Fostering a unified company culture!

- You have access to a platform through your Smart Campus app that enables employees to remain connected, productive, and content with their daily lives.

- The battle for talent is genuine, as any manager who has attempted to hire an employee will attest. Free lunches and on-site laundry are no longer acceptable job benefits.

- Every business needs to improve its work in order to attract talent in today's market. On-site or hybrid work has returned to many businesses, but I don't believe the rigid work schedule will ever be reinstated.
- You've learned over the past two years that although in-person and real-time interactions are extremely useful, many other jobs can be completed asynchronously just as well or perhaps better.
- Flexibility is now a must thanks to a strong digital basis. Let your staff determine where, when, and how to provide what is required of them.
- You might also try to impose a tight work paradigm and watch as your best employees leave for another company.
- Nobody is claiming that your workplace must be the most costly or opulent. But it should be a top concern to ensure that the equipment is current and working.
- You don't want an employee's valuable time being squandered wrangling with a printer that ought to have been discarded in the vast sky-based junkyard ten years ago.
- While you now understand that you cannot control everyone's living conditions, you can manage the tools your company provides to employees who work from home.
- Your employees won't go ignored if you opt to offer ergonomic desks and chairs or frequent check-ins on how systems are running.
- Progress may not necessarily include reward or financial gain. Yes, many of you find that wage raises and bonuses are really motivating. However, individuals also desire to be appreciated, acknowledged, and rewarded at work.

- A thorough learning and development program not only enables your employees to advance their skills and explore their interests, but also demonstrates to them your willingness to devote time and resources to their personal development. According to Gallup, 87% of millennials agree that chances for learning and growth play a significant role in determining whether they take a new job or not.

Are there individuals presently employed by your company who may be given a shot if you are recruiting? Are there any skill gaps you might cover by allowing a member of your team to try out?

It's critical to keep in mind that your teams have lives outside of your company. Ensuring everyone has adequate free time to engage in their hobbies outside of work is a crucial component of developing a positive, healthy workplace culture.

- In a poll, it is discovered that younger workers experience greater apprehension and trepidation while conducting these difficult talks. The most worried group was the millennial generation, with 84% saying they felt apprehensive about talking to their bosses at work. It's especially important for managers and supervisors of younger employees to maintain these conversations and foster work settings where team members feel comfortable sharing problems or asking for assistance.
- Establishing goals The effectiveness of the wellness program depends on setting health objectives that are advantageous to both the organisation and the workforce.

- Forming a team is important since it will be responsible for organising and carrying out the wellness program. Members of the team should come from all organisational areas.
- The wellness program's design determines how it will be implemented. At this point, budgets are made, research is done on concepts, and staff needs are identified.
- Regular feedback, as well as making any necessary corrections or modifications, is critical for the success of the wellness program.
- The easiest approach to getting things going is to establish clear expectations early on and provide teams with all the resources they need to lead these open and frequent discussions. For content teams, these tools and technologies have become standard.
- By fostering an atmosphere of open communication, everyone will feel heard and be able to take on new responsibilities with confidence.
- The typical employee works about 50 hours each week and consumes around one-third of their meals there.
- Organisations must adopt a more comprehensive perspective on their employees' wellness if they want to change the culture of the organisation and make it more meaningful.

There are a few crucial things to keep in mind about the necessity of corporate wellness: "Organisations with highly effective health and productivity programs report 11% more revenue per employee, 1.8 fewer days absent per employee per year, and 28% larger shareholder returns." Employers who offer wellness programs report higher employee satisfaction, higher productivity, more financial sustainability and development, and lower absenteeism in 50% of cases.

"People desire a better work environment, and if they don't receive it, they'll take their skills elsewhere."

If an employer uses "substandard" technology, 42% of millennials are likely to leave that position. Productivity is increased by 18% with a second monitor. Some employees find that standing while they work increases their comfort, concentration, and productivity. Therefore, even if the standup work configuration just saves 10 minutes each day, the added productivity would equal one work week annually. Any business that wants to flourish has to be proactive about employee welfare. Through programs like meditation and mindfulness classes, wellness speeches, staff fitness drives, etc., wellbeing must be incorporated into an organisation as a constant drive and activity.

"Workplace health is still a top issue for corporate success and continuity in the rapidly changing environment and times you live in."

Yoga provides a lot of health advantages. It is a useful approach to include self-care, and doing it at work ensures that the body is physiologically capable of handling any difficulties. Activities that foster better bonds amongst coworkers, such as organising book clubs and game evenings, are examples of virtual social activities that can improve workplace morale. Important elements for carrying out wellness initiatives Employers must take certain actions that focus on the following when implementing workplace wellness programs. Despite the fact that 55% of workers say they are most productive at their desks, 20 to 25% of US workers regularly work remotely. Collaboration and a more effective exchange of ideas can be facilitated by reevaluating the function of the workplace and designing flexible workspaces. An IT service provider might act as a partner by helping a business determine its needs and create a deployment strategy.

- Provide constructive criticism using the CSS-Continue, Start, Stop methodology. Using this approach to structure your feedback will enable you to highlight the employee's strengths and areas for improvement. Although receiving feedback and having the capacity to comprehend employee problems are crucial, retention ultimately depends on what you do afterwards.

- Always be open and honest by disclosing your findings and a plan of action for solving the problem. As an illustration, following a recent company-wide engagement survey, you decided to inform all workers of the results.

- You shared not just our greatest successes but also our areas for growth and our future plans for addressing them. Transparent communication and a straightforward "we heard you" may both be very helpful.

- Increased vacation days should be given to your top performers. These workers are your superstars, so you can be sure they'll finish their tasks and take a few more days off to be with friends and family.

- The aim is to make everyone informed and direct them in the same direction. Giving everyone as much responsibility, opportunity, and recognition as they desire is the plan of attack for achieving that objective. Since rank-and-file employees are the ones performing the work on the ground, they sometimes lack an overview of the company's operations. It might be challenging for them to understand how their job advances the goals of the business.

- Inform employees clearly and frequently about how their individual responsibilities fit into the overall objective.
- Alignment with the organisation's goal should start during the hiring process and extend through the whole onboarding and training process.
- Don't stop there, though. Remind team members frequently how their daily efforts further the mission. Not broadly speaking. Give them concrete, precise instances.
- Instruct managers to incorporate "mission moments" into team meetings. Embrace the purpose and values in your employee evaluations.
- Create a monthly employee spotlight film that highlights a particular individual, group, or position and how their present work furthers the purpose.
- Companies should take action to provide areas where staff members may readily communicate and share ideas. Informal interactions in the break room can develop into productive ones. If you can, add good furniture, tables, food, and drinks to make it effective and welcoming.

Another area where business choices are frequently made in solitude is this one. They choose to hold an out-of-office function or a team-building day. Without ever consulting the employee, they come up with a concept and plan it. This strategy is well known in the military. So-called "mandated fun days" are these. It does so sometimes. It falters sometimes. But even if it doesn't end up being very enjoyable, individuals will nearly always be happier with a corporate outing if they had a hand in organising it. Asking your staff what they want to accomplish is the easy option. The secret is to create boundaries. If not, you could come up with some very absurd ideas. Make sure everyone is aware of the schedule, the travel requirements (or restrictions) for attendees, and the financial constraints. After gathering suggestions, pick the best one and make a video announcement informing the team of the details (this method also applies to virtual events!). Remember to thank everyone who contributed to inspire others to submit their ideas the next time you organise an event.

- You discovered that giving employees who don't think there are exciting career options for them within the firm developmental support—like training opportunities and career mentoring—leads to such people quitting the organisation.
- It's crucial for organisations to regularly discuss career planning with their staff. Make sure employees are aware of the many career pathways or employment prospects within the organisation as part of training and development.
- Pay attention to your employees' complaints and issues, then provide solutions. Your employees ought to feel heard and confident in their abilities. When faced with difficulties, your employees should feel certain that they will be listened to and supported. This will solidify your relationship with them and give them a sense of support and concern.

"The adage, "Praise openly, criticise quietly," or any version of it, may have been repeated to you."

It's straightforward counsel that works. But how frequently do you truly heed such counsel? Normal workplaces influence us to provide praise and feedback in the worst conceivable ways. It comes naturally to offer someone a quick high-five at their office or after a meeting. And discussing issues in a group context is very normal. Private feedback is something you all need to practise. But there is a lot HR teams and managers can do to foster a climate of open adoration. An organisation-wide praise system is simple to put into place. With a whiteboard in the break room or "high-five" moments during all-staff meetings, you can go old-school, but why not step it up a level with brief thanks videos that commend employees for their hard work?

There are many business issues that need to be resolved in any organisation but may not be the responsibility of a particular team or person. Upper management is frequently given the task of solving these issues. Each business, however, also employs a large number of intelligent, inventive individuals. And a lot of these folks are eager to lend a hand if given the chance.

Group brainstorming is a tried-and-true method for involving the entire team. It's also a fantastic approach to fixing issues. Group brainstorming, however, necessitates yet another gathering. Additionally, it is innately blind to quieter but no less important voices. Instead, take a chance and issue a general call for suggestions from the staff.

- Reward them for their efforts with compliments, cash incentives, promotions, prizes, and so on.
- Remember that encouraging words, bonuses, and awards for going above and beyond may all significantly increase job satisfaction.

- Recognise an employee's efforts if they are successful. Your staff members work alongside you, not for you.
- To build a team of contented, driven employees, you'll need to be able to treat everyone equally and with respect. Instead of just telling your staff to do what you say, learn to work with them.
- Develop a better workplace culture where your employees can feel appreciated, respected, and motivated.
- It is obvious that not every employee has to be knowledgeable about every facet of a company. However, individuals enjoy being privy to knowledge and feeling part of a trusted group.
- Employees feel more trusted by the organisation when they are informed of a few things that take place in the C-suite behind closed doors. When a new rule is introduced, explain the rationale for the change (to the extent possible).
- In keeping with this, let employees know where the business is going and what difficulties management is tackling. An easy and efficient method to achieve this is to provide videos of periodic update reports. With a team trial, you may enable editing.
- Assist brand-new team members in establishing connections. The fact that members of remote teams sometimes feel as though they don't know one another presents one of the greatest difficulties.
- When your main communication with your peers is through email, Slack chats, and sporadic video calls, it's easy to feel alone. Each new team member at my consultancy is required to produce a brief self-introduction video before the end of their first week. Each new team member at my consultancy is required

to make a little video introducing themselves before the end of their first week and post it on Slack.

- You have discovered that it helps both the existing team members and new team members give a voice and a face to the emails and communications. Both remote and in-person employees can introduce themselves in this sort of film in a unique style that doesn't make them nervous about speaking in front of an audience.

- Provide employees with a template for a "meet the team" video to make it simple. Editing is available after a team trial.

- Utilise employee expertise while developing new training.

- Giving employees the chance to pursue outside training and certifications is extremely beneficial for both employee engagement and employee competency. However, the majority of businesses also have a vast knowledge base within their workforce.

- Unfortunately, most information is passed casually from employee to employee when someone is stuck or having trouble with something. It lacks clarity and effectiveness.

- Encouragement of employees to host formal internal training to assist in upskilling the rest of the team based on the difficulties they encounter on a daily basis is a preferable strategy. This offers competent workers the chance to assume additional responsibility if they so want. Additionally, it helps your teams disseminate information before work becomes stagnant.

- Incentive programs are frequently created utilising a formulaic methodology. And it's widely believed that money is the best motivation. An excellent motivation is money. However, it's not always the ideal motivator.

Keep in mind that workers may be content with their wages yet still be miserable. Depending on what employees value the most, an effective incentive program may not entail any direct spending at all. The ideal incentive may be for certain workers to be allowed to go early one or two days each week, provided that all the jobs are completed.

- Another employee's motivation may be increased if they are given a half-hour to exercise or work on personal projects each day. The best approach could be to provide tangible rewards. But unless you inquire, you won't know.

- Crowdsource concepts for your incentive programs much like how you crowdsource answers to difficult situations. Post a little video. Inform everyone that you need their assistance to establish or improve your incentive programs. You may even say that you're seeking alternatives to monetary rewards to receive a wider range of suggestions.

The company's goals are often achieved by content employees since they are the only ones who take the time to learn about these goals in the first place. When workers are content, they are more motivated to work and feel involved in the organisation's objectives. Since more involvement results in happier workers who are more present, happiness boosts productivity. They are more aware of the company's systems and procedures, and they focus more on the demands of the consumers. Together, these elements help organisations become more productive and profitable.

According to Gallup, contented workers are more resilient and more likely to stick with their employers over the long run. A reduced turnover implies fewer breaks or productivity slowdowns while also requiring less time and money to find, hire, and train new employees. Additionally, content workers make it a point to come in and do extra work. They find it simpler to work longer hours and go above and beyond what is required of them. Remember that gratitude fosters loyalty.

According to a recent poll by Boston Consulting Group, the majority of individuals just desire one thing—appreciation for their work—from their employers. Who makes the effort to hunt for a new job when they enjoy the one they have and are appreciated there?

- Create a volunteer goal, such as volunteering 1,000 hours at local groups by the end of the year, if your company, for example, takes pride in its involvement in the community. Every time an employee donates their time, they may record their efforts in a shared software that shows the overall progress completed and how far there is still to go.
- Offering group awards to the departments or teams who go above and beyond their share of the task can motivate your staff and promote happiness. Employees will have a stronger connection to and appreciation for their job when they can see how their efforts positively improve both your company and their neighborhood.
- Innovation is the lifeblood of every company, and only content people have the motivation to think creatively and come up with the answers your organisation requires. While unsatisfied workers are more likely to play it safe, happy workers are more willing to take sensible chances.

- Taking advantage of the appropriate opportunities at the right time is the key to success in business, and motivated people are more likely to spot and address holes in the market or your organisation's operations.
- Additionally, contented workers provide a supportive environment at work that encourages everyone to learn from their mistakes rather than to avoid them. Employees who are hesitant to make errors risk missing out on crucial learning opportunities. Mistakes may be a valuable learning tool that can lead to unexpected success.

You can promote yourself as a fun place to work if you can. However, it doesn't just occur. You and your organisation must decide. You may take is to express your hiring criteria in detail to potential candidates. Tell them you're looking for employees who want to join a great organisation and are engaged, eager, and driven. Describe a facet of your company's culture to them. Make it plain that you won't put up with mediocrity or disinterest.

You're looking for those that are extremely motivated and give it their all every day at work. If you're ready to rock, "You're the place for you," as you have a high-productivity and high-engagement culture that's not for someone looking for a comfort zone. Who wouldn't want to work in such an environment? Possessing a strong employee referral program is another option. The best prospects are found through referrals, whether the reference sources are current or former coworkers, customers, suppliers, or others.

Make sure your referral sources are aware of your particular needs. After that, give the referral process some energy. By providing links or materials that candidates may use, you can assist your sources. I will then determine the best way to thank them for the recommendation. As a result, I'm challenging you to take a close look at your hiring strategies and consider how you might apply these concepts to start luring in excellent prospects right away.

Finally, take into account the possible employees' geographic and functional mobility. Your best talents are often those who have the flexibility to relocate where the job is and are willing to learn new skills or take on new positions in today's volatile, unpredictable, complex, conflict, ambiguous, and dynamism (VUCCAD) world and global economy. It's crucial to periodically evaluate these elements. At some point in their career, not everyone is geographically or functionally movable.

"The value of intangible assets, including brand recognition, expertise, invention, and notably human capital, is being highlighted by a new economic paradigm that is defined by speed, innovation, short cycle times, quality, and customer happiness. A golden era for HR may have begun with the introduction of this new paradigm."-Dr. Amit Das

CHAPTER TWO

Cultivating A Happier And Productive Work Environment

"Research indicates that workers have three prime needs: Interesting work, recognition for doing a good job, and being let in on things that are going on in the organisation." - Zig Ziglar

As you have entered the third year of the epidemic, soft skills have taken centre stage in the talent competition. They have usually been ignored or rejected when judging corporate executives. In order to support the workforce, HR executives must help managers acquire the abilities they need to handle challenging dialogues that foster team cohesiveness, inclusiveness, and psychological safety. This necessitates educating managers on how to handle delicate situations and customise their communication with each person in order to fully understand their motivations and behaviours.

A new set of options for closing skills gaps emerges with the increased capabilities that AI, cognitive computing, and robots will unleash. Any connection, including one at work, is similar. A little give and a little take. Although it may seem unnecessary, by supporting your employees' professional growth, you will create a culture of empowerment and benefit when they excitedly put their newly acquired talents to use.

Make sure you have the resources available to make learning enjoyable and convenient. To demonstrate to your team that you are prepared to invest in their ongoing, daily learning, think about using current learning and development tools.

Agility, the capacity to adapt to change, fast learning, and interpersonal skills are some of the most frequently identified traits as possible development areas. Resilience is the capacity to use creativity to overcome challenges, recover from failure, and keep one's equilibrium. Creativity is the capacity to tackle issues in novel and creative ways and to create new goods or approaches. Drive is the desire to advance professionally and accomplish great things. The term "intellect" refers to a person's broad cognitive ability, which includes the capability to think critically about a wide range of topics and act promptly in challenging circumstances.

Entrepreneurship is the capacity to start a new organisation from scratch with a concept or an idea and grow it into a profitable operation. Let's examine a case in point. Consider that your organisation is getting ready to restructure its business model significantly in order to deploy a new go-to-market approach. Of them, which three would you pick?

An excellent and effective strategy to encourage a collaborative sharing culture is to develop knowledge management systems. HR departments must reconsider their knowledge management systems as we transition to the digital era. If they select the right application, they will be able to simplify the sorts of functions they use every day. The organisation of files, folders, emails, and calendars is made possible by a low-cost, readily scalable knowledge-sharing platform. Whether they are in the same office or working remotely, it also makes it simple for team members to collaborate on content and other activities. The options are endless right now!

Organisations can, for instance, concentrate on a single talent to identify the training that will improve that skill the most. For knowledge-based skills, this is very useful. It is suggested that information on behavioral and coaching programs be offered for soft skills, including teamwork and delegation.

Organisations may also assess where L & D projects are most successful at creating skills and where they are not using the growing amount of data. Even though there are now few organisations that have a comprehensive skill-taxonomy, the sector is quickly developing. Both specialized suppliers and significant businesses are working on skill taxonomy, skill inference, and level ratings. As a result, people analytics has significant potential to help bridge the talent gap.

You chose the traits of drive, entrepreneurism, and resilience for this example because you want leaders who have a strong desire to achieve, who can take an idea and run with it, and who won't be discouraged by obstacles in their path. You can choose a different set of considerations if you intend to undergo a merger or reorganisation in the coming years. To restructure your organisation, you should probably search for executives that are intelligent, agile, and creative. Knowing the direction your organisation is taking can help you identify the best components or possible elements to achieve the outcomes you desire. Begin with the objective in mind once more.

Create the criteria for your program. You've reached a thrilling point. The development of your top talent program should begin now. You might just choose employees for your program based on the advice of their managers. But how can you be certain that the standards used to choose them are impartial and that you don't miss any untapped potential? I'll share a well-kept secret with you. To find individuals to take part in the top talent program, the majority of businesses use a nomination procedure. The best strategy to select your participants is to hold a strict nomination procedure for this reason.

Based on the probable variables and other criteria you've chosen, the first stage in establishing your nomination process is figuring out who can nominate someone and what information you'll require. The process, the personnel, and the timetable are the next three main factors to be chosen. What criteria will you use to evaluate the nominees? Who will choose the nominees for best talent? And when are the nomination, evaluation, and development procedures expected to be finished?

As you can see, there are several factors that need to be chosen. Before producing a thorough strategy, I strongly advise generating an outline or executive summary with suggested solutions and presenting it to your key stakeholders. You'll get the support you'll need later to make sure your program runs smoothly and meets its objectives by making the process more open and collaborative. Later, during the calibration step, you will be able to reduce the pool. Imagine it as a talent funnel. When evaluating candidates for a talent program, businesses consider a range of factors. The most frequently utilized variables, in addition to potential, are time with the organisation or time in the current function; previous and present performance; habits; and mobility.

Additionally, a beneficial trend in recent years is that managers and employees are increasingly at ease working remotely. Take a look at their readiness and capacity to implement these changes successfully. Although I covered a lot, you now have a strong framework for the design of your program and the important work that lies ahead. By setting rather strict criteria for nomination, you may avoid discouraging individuals from suggesting prospective talent while also forcing employees and supervisors to deliberate over their suggestions. You should eventually have 1% to 2% of your total workforce. The criteria for nomination should then be very explicit in order to exclude any room for confusion.

When it comes to things involving individuals, there will always be some subjectivity and hidden agendas. So it's beneficial to use the most impartial criterion you can. You utilised the following standards in one organisation where I oversaw the design and implementation of a top talent program: The nominee must have been employed by our organisation and performing the duties of their present position for at least one year, preferably two years, and must have met or surpassed the goals set out in their annual performance review. This criterion was selected because you wanted to include folks who are already contributing well but may be able to do even better.

You are requested specific examples of the nominee's past success and potential from the nominating party. Mobility is a significant potential area. Think about candidates who will be geographically or functionally movable during the next one to two years so they may grow and learn about your organisation's business by working in different environments. This demonstrates a person's capacity for growth as well as their readiness to be adaptable and step outside of their comfort zone. Let's spend a little more time discussing mobility. Not everyone is career-mobile at all times. For a number of reasons, including family, education, and income, some people are now unable to migrate. But bear in mind that they could move about in the future.

Fortunately, you've grown much more accustomed to working remotely, so nowadays, moving physically is not the only choice. It is beneficial to take into account additional factors, such as functional mobility. Consider giving a financial professional a year in a field sales management job to develop them. Finally, the issue of who can make a nomination arises.

Should it just be the manager of the individual, the manager of the person's manager, or a peer?

Sometimes the rebels or mavericks—those who are normally challenging to manage and might not get favourable performance reviews—are the ones that have the greatest potential for you. These could be some of your really top abilities, though. You now have it. I can tell you that from a lot of information, so I advise you to run your nomination criteria by one or two of your stakeholders once you've created them to make sure you're on the same page and have their support. On to your meetings for talent assessment now. Collect and arrange the nomination data. You've organised, shared, and begun your nomination process by this point, and you've already had a lot of nominations, suggesting a lot of interest in your program.

Although I recognise how wonderful it is, how do you manage everything? You must establish a method to classify the data you get. I promise that if you understand this straight away, the calibration step will be a lot simpler for you to handle. Human Resources Information Systems (often known as HRIS) are widely used in many companies and enable businesses to collect and arrange all the data relating to their personnel in an organisation-wide database.

In order to generate a wider skills universe, organisations must construct an ecosystem where numerous stakeholders share responsibility for various aspects of the skills pie. This ecosystem must include tasks that organisations, employees, and training institutions must do. Learning will transition from being mass produced to being tailored to the needs of the individual employee, allowing for more intimate integration of work and learning, expanding ownership of learning beyond the HR division and exploring ways to apply solutions you use in your daily lives to the learning environment at work. It's important to unlearn one-dimensional learning paths and create person-based growth pathways. You must begin considering matrix careers and giving people opportunities to explore new things. Organisations must plan a step-by-step process to include these components in their learning strategy. This process includes understanding and developing career paths using a role matrix and role dictionary; skill mapping for each role; evaluating candidates for both current and future roles; and implementing skill development programs.

You now possess the information and resources necessary to successfully design and manage your top talent program. The moment has come for you to implement your strategy in order to recognise and maximize your best skills. Show your business how to place these top individuals so they may realize their full potential and support the expansion and profitability of the enterprise. Use this top talent pool to fill the most important and strategic jobs for your business, and keep the process going to maintain your talent pool current.

Great companies attract employees, so they don't need to look for them. Candidates of the highest calibre are lined up to apply to companies like Southwest Airlines, KPMG, and Zappos. Organisations like Southwest Airlines have reaped the benefits of the "employee first" philosophy in spades. Employees are more willing to go above and beyond to prioritise the needs of the and its customers when they share in the profits, as is the case at Southwest. In 2017, Southwest distributed $586 million to its workforce, or six weeks' worth of compensation for each employee.

It's hardly surprising that the business keeps reporting record earnings. What method do they employ? They add interest to the whole employment process. These days, people are frequently eager to establish themselves in order to develop quickly when they join a new organisation or job. Even if they have promise in the future, it's crucial to assess how well they provide or perform before selecting them for a top talent program. Before being nominated, most businesses prefer that candidates have a one-to two-year track record. Many businesses today take an employee's habits into account when evaluating their overall performance. They consider how a person achieves her objectives and whether her actions are in line with the organisation's ideals.

How to build a learning ecosystem in your organisation?

During the course of a year or two, many of your skills may get promoted or depart the organisation. Since it's not ideal to shift individuals more frequently than once a year, not even your top performers. A top talent is typically taken from the top talent pool after being promoted to assess how they perform at their new level. As a result, you will eventually need to completely replenish your pool. I say sometimes because, if you do your formal top talent program every two years, you should be aware that, for the reasons already mentioned, your pool will eventually shrink and that, before you run your process again, new people with more potential will appear. To identify prospective top talent and maybe evaluate and develop them before the formal process begins again, it's important to have constant communication with both human resources experts who work directly with companies and business leaders themselves.

"Employees feel appreciated and encouraged to perform their best job when they have access to ongoing learning and development opportunities"

Be alert to any upcoming adjustments to the workforce or organisation that could create a need for unique skills or abilities to fill a particular position. Within two to three years, 80% to 90% of your top performers will have lost their status, either because they were promoted, left the organisation, or met or fell short of their expected potential for a variety of reasons. As a result, you must restart your official top talent program. The good news is that you now have all the information you need to get ready for your program's next revision.

Additionally, you have the benefit of experience, which enables you to participate in that program knowing the significant effects it has already had on your organisation. You can now, I believe, safely declare that you are an expert in managing a top talent program. Implement your top talent program.

"In a world where money is no longer the primary motivating factor for employees, focusing on the employee experience is the most promising competitive advantage that organisations can create." -Jacob Morgan

The current organisational focus must be on providing people with the skills they need to improve performance both now and in the future. In order to adjust to a new normal and a hybrid future where a combination of remote working and office attendance will revolutionise the workplace, businesses are cautiously preparing for the return of a portion of their employees to offices. Since approximately 85 million jobs are anticipated to be automated in the next five years, the World Economic Forum's Global Risks Report 2021 states that the most crucial objective for HR directors would be to meet the changing skill demands.

"Businesses will gain a lot from upskilling and technology in the hybrid world."

People increasingly prioritise the "chance to learn" as one of their top considerations when accepting a job, according to Deloitte Insights. Leaders are aware of the tremendous need for ongoing learning that has been created by changes in technology, longevity, work habits, and business structures. Companies' learning and development departments have been essential during the epidemic, and their L&D expenditures have climbed dramatically and are expected to do so again soon.

By reorganising organisational objectives and labor strategies, many organisations are already laying the groundwork for the future. According to a McKinsey Global poll published in February 2020, 87% of executives feel there is a talent gap in their staff, but they are unclear about how to fix it. Since the pandemic's onset, uncertainty has persisted, which has led to agility in upskilling and reskilling taking centre stage.

However, organisations are now investing in their employees' learning to counteract the skill gap. 54% of the world's workforce will require reskilling and upskilling by 2022, according to recent industry statistics, and given the current circumstances, the focus is only going to grow in the years to come. Businesses that are successful will make investments in their employees' upskilling and reskilling as well as in more strategically managing both long-term career development and day-to-day work experience, while also making sure that they are in line with corporate goals.

Whether or not there is a pandemic, one must learn to adapt to the hyper-competitive age by offering much more. The growth of workers will also depend heavily on their social, soft, and emotional abilities. HR directors must provide employees more opportunities to acquire new skills, let go of outdated ones, and reskill while utilising innovative teaching strategies.

Skills like empathy and decision-making, in addition to creativity, critical thinking, intellectual curiosity, and innovation, will be in high demand among organisations. Employers and employees will need to position themselves in a way that emphasises adaptability along with persistence.

Do you know about talent bench?

It is now necessary to prioritise talent data and look beyond bottlenecks. Most organisations have extensive knowledge of their workforce but less knowledge of their talent pool. Organisations have been required by law and government regulations to retain employee and personnel data in perfect shape, and the HR Information Systems (HRIS) designed to meet these requirements have developed dramatically. Are businesses able to obtain employee numbers that are segmented by tenure, experience level, or geography? Yes, over and over. For example, employee experience across competences or abilities, positions held during tenure, and even certain fundamental productivity measurements like work hours and effort, especially for knowledge and service sectors, make it challenging when it is necessary to dig deeper.

As if this weren't difficult enough, the pandemic necessitates more real-time data, such as a worker's current location when operating remotely, the status of their health checks and vaccinations, their work schedules and availability, and so on.The majority of organisations have not yet built real-time visibility into their HRIS.

Additionally, they could have a talent management system with integrated software that organises this data. These would be perfect for organising your nominations. Working with an HRIS is simple. You'll need to develop a logic to extract the data you want from the database of your business and organise it in a way that is useful. In order to ease the process of inputting and extracting the data you need in a usable manner, communicate this reasoning and the associated business needs with your information technology department so they may modify or adjust the HRIS and talent management software, if applicable. However, many businesses are either too tiny or don't have the necessary technological sophistication to use these kinds of solutions.

Is employees' reluctance to share data to blame for the gap in data availability?

According to a new survey , the majority of employees 70% are prepared to provide vital information about themselves if there is anything in it for them. However, the report is particularly specific to personal health information. For instance, the majority of employees, especially Millennials, would be prepared to share work hours and flexible-hour patterns if doing so would assist the organisation in discovering the best-suited project. When compared to the Gen X cohort of respondents, who were far less enthusiastic about sharing knowledge, a closer look at the demographics of this survey reveals that 79% of Millennials will share information if they have any takeaways.

Therefore, it is safe to say that if purpose and value are created, workers are not obstacles to data availability. It's time to face the truth and look inward now that all likely suspects have been eliminated from the list. Most businesses give less priority to talent data because the return on investment of a capable and reliable talent information system is difficult to measure. Because a talent information system must be very contextual, which makes the purchasing process challenging, starting from scratch is the best option. The data source is not as clear-cut as, for example, data obtained from a job application.

Talent information frequently exists within the limits of natural conversations between team members and management. It can also appear as "value additions" like gratitude notes, carefully concealed as a brand-new ability picked up on the job, or in other hidden treasures. The first step in getting everything in order and taking control of talent data is choosing and working with either an internal IT team that is well-equipped or a technology partner who comprehends the business context and has the breadth of experience and resources necessary to build the talent data solution that the organisation and employees require.

How to build a positive work culture in your organisation?

It's crucial to establish a culture that will both maximise your employees' abilities and keep the rest of your crew motivated. People who weren't chosen for the program will cooperate more to ensure the success of the organisation once they realise the benefits to themselves. Top talent is crucial since they can acquire the abilities required to advance into prominent positions within your organisation. These few responsibilities in every organisation that, if unfilled for even a short period of time, would seriously harm that organisation's performance, financial results, or reputation are known as mission essential positions. From the Chief Executive Officer, or CEO, through general managers and sales leaders, these jobs encompass a whole organisation. Everything depends on how big and how organized your business is. Investment analysts frequently give a organisation's human or intellectual capital a high level of relevance and worth. The strength of the leadership team and the breadth and calibre of the organisation's talent pool are two factors that are taken into consideration when businesses, venture capitalists, and private equity organisations explore mergers or acquisitions. The future success of an organisation depends on its capacity to recognise and develop these people's potential.

A further challenge is getting individuals to work productively. You conducted a final conference when the whole leadership team, including the president, debated and decided the final ranking of the talents who had been rated highest in earlier sessions, once all of these talent calibration meetings were finished and the candidates calibrated. You may now understand why I mentioned at the outset that this aspect of the procedure was exceedingly difficult. I also mentioned the necessity for preparation in order to successfully plan talent assessment meetings and choose the top people for your business. And you do now.

When you're prepared to conduct your talent calibration meetings, this will presumably be one of the most exciting phases of your top talent program. The actual action starts here, and it may get really fierce at times. Why do you suppose I call the meetings tense? It's because the managers who make the nominations typically bring a lot of emotion to the meetings since they have high expectations for and strong beliefs in the candidates. You must be well-prepared and have the information in order if you intend to lead these sessions yourself. Above all, keep composed and rational when the conversations become heated. Your major objectives should be to have fruitful talks that result in an accurate assessment of your abilities and the identification of top talent for your organisation.

In a talent calibration meeting, all of these considerations would be used to showcase and evaluate the candidate's potential. You now have it. You may successfully submit your nominations if you put a little effort and imagination into the design of your profile. And you're one step closer to developing a worthwhile program to recognize and nurture your best skills. Differentiate between performance and potential. Being able to distinguish between performance and potential in an impartial manner is one of the most difficult and occasionally perplexing parts of evaluating talent. To help you understand the differences between these, let's look at them more closely.

The easiest one is the last one, because almost everyone likes to be thanked for their contributions. Recognising everyone's contribution is difficult. It's easy to concentrate on the top performers and the exceptional home runs, but it's also crucial to acknowledge those who might not immediately jump out. The worker that constantly turns up and completes their task on schedule also merits praise for their dependability. In other words, give praise freely. And make sure that everyone gets credited for their contributions.

The other long-term advantage is that your organisation, especially its leaders, can establish a shared understanding and vocabulary to identify and discuss one of its most important resources, its top talent, through the talent calibration sessions. To get the participants ready for the talent-calibration sessions, you created and delivered targeted training. To give the managers a realistic idea of what to expect, you organized webinars, Q&A sessions, and even made several movies with roleplays of fake calibration conversations. I have to admit that you still didn't fully prepare them. Once they were seated side by side in the room, it was a very different experience.

The culture of the particular group you were meeting with and how well the participants knew the nominees had a big impact on some fascinating group dynamics. Because certain groups were so close-knit, it was difficult for them to distinguish between the talents under consideration because they didn't want to question or irritate the other managers or run the danger of harming the careers of the talents. Some supervisors questioned the talents' qualifications in other groups a little too vehemently. In all instances, I had to stay impartial and intervene to guide the conversations in the right direction. Asking the participants to concentrate more on potential than performance and not whether they personally liked or hated the talent being reviewed was another difficulty for me. They found it far simpler to discuss the talents' past accomplishments or the reasons why they were likeable than to discuss what they may be capable of.

It also greatly increases the severity of your procedure. One talent at a calibration meeting seemed to have more potential than her boss had given her credit for. The manager acknowledged undervaluing her since she was in a crucial position and the manager couldn't afford to lose her when the CEO pressed the issue. After that, you had a constructive conversation about the significance of appropriately identifying abilities that may benefit the organisation as a whole and not holding real talents back. In the end, you may plan 10 conferences over a three-month period and discover roughly 30 individuals that may have hastened the growth of your business. I've given you my example because I want you to understand how it could feel and what effect you might have after doing your calibration meetings effectively.

It's crucial to obtain the appropriate mixture since structuring and managing the nomination process may be a very difficult task. How come, in your opinion? You'll need the right individuals in the mix from the start if you want to operate an efficient top talent program that will discover the employees with the most potential in your organisation. Therefore, there shouldn't be too many or too few of them.

Additionally, by integrating those who don't really jump out as having apparent abilities, it's possible to uncover some hidden gems. Running a successful nomination process is the only way you can do this. Let's see how you can accomplish that. You had to accomplish this manually using spreadsheets since one of the organisations. This may take a long time and will require a lot of work.

However, after you used a system you came up with to arrange the spreadsheets, you were able to retrieve the data quite quickly. And before the nomination season started, you set this up. So, when the nominations began to roll in, you were totally ready. You would have been in trouble if you had waited until the nominations started to come in. You produced a one-page visual biography of each nominee for each nomination you got that contained the most crucial details, such as their tenure with the organisation and in their current position, performance evaluations, and the sorts of projects or cross-functional experience they've worked on.

Are you prepared to think about the possibility of creating the best employees in your organisation?

Prepare yourself to create a top talent program. When the circumstances are ideal and you have executive sponsorship, successfully executing a top talent program will be advantageous to your organisation in many ways. A significant cultural change program was also devised to aid in the implementation of the new plan.

In order to prevent a disruption of operations in these crucial sectors, they lacked a talent pipeline ready to fill these roles swiftly. The terrible experience of lacking top employees at a crucial moment taught the CEO a valuable lesson. He maintained that the creation of a top talent program had to be a component of the attempt to alter the culture, and the business was in a position to pay for it.

Can you imagine how this situation might have played out if the business had a system in place to recognise its best employees?

It's now your chance to consider how establishing a top talent program to find and nurture high-potential people during the upcoming year can assist your business. Even the most capable millennials from elite institutions are powerless to affect any qualitative or quantitative change in their organisation in the absence of a commensurate infrastructure.

Many top executives frequently profess their fervent desire to bring new energy to their organisations. The demand-supply balance for talent in India is often favourable to employers, especially in the knowledge sector, and this situation is anticipated to persist in the foreseeable future. On the contrary, it is a good idea to take into account the demographic change in India as well as the vigour and enthusiasm that millennials bring with them. After all, it is the next generation of workers who will shape organisations' futures and encourage the implementation of agile succession techniques.

This, however, only tells part of the story because most businesses struggle to create what might be described as a "matching infrastructure" for their young workers. Matching Infrastructure refers to the total supportive environment made up of material and intangible structures and procedures that are essential for maximising and using the potential of millennials. In a straightforward comparison, our body has a system of veins, arteries, and a heart that allows blood to execute its intended activities. If this system is absent or malfunctions, blood stagnates regardless of the amounts of haemoglobin and other essential components. Similar to this, even the most skilled millennials from top-tier institutions are unable to affect any qualitative or quantitative change in their organisation in the absence of a corresponding infrastructure. Organisations must understand that terminology like "Millennial" or "Gen Z," etc., is more than just semantics. In reality, they demonstrate a fundamental shift in how people think and act. This generation is accustomed to quick actions and outcomes, free-flowing knowledge, and empowerment and independent thought.

You now know who your organisation's best employees are. So what comes next? How will you handle them? You create them. Keep in mind that the goal of your program is to find and support the individuals who can have the most influence on your business. There are two ways you can aid in their development. Give them opportunities that are difficult and will push their existing limits. You may provide them with a variety of learning and self-development resources, like executive education or training courses, the opportunity to work with a coach or mentor, and this is empowerment. They can be enabled in these ways. Consider how you can provide development to the cohort as a whole, meet their needs as a group, foster a leadership community within the cohort, and tailor development to individual unique developmental areas.

"We need to ask ourselves what we need to do to stay relevant in the future. I don't believe you can do very much wrong at this moment in time because it's never been tested. The only thing you can do is you can experience that this is probably not the right thing to do and change, try something new."

-Peter Baumann, SAP

I'll provide a few of my experiences as examples. In one top talent program I oversaw, you utilised psychometric tests to benchmark or contrast the best talent in your organisation with talent in other organisations of the same calibre. One of the things you learned was that, in comparison to your rivals, your top employees lacked the capacity to operationalise your approach. They were conceptualising and understanding the organisation's plan, but they weren't carrying it out as well as they might have. You thus concentrated on providing your top talents with assignments that needed them to establish a plan to implement a certain business strategy as part of the group development plan. This was the part about empowering people, and to accomplish this, you offered them new skills like training in design thinking. This was the portion that enabled You did note, however, that some individuals were successful in carrying out strategy but still needed development in the area of interpersonal relations.

How to create a great employee value proposition?

Individual Development Plans, or IDPs, with 360-degree feedback and the chance to interact with coaches were created for these elite performers. This was the portion that enabled Through project leadership responsibilities, you offered them the chance to practise the people skills they had gained from the coaching and feedback. The part that empowered you was this.You were able to identify and meet the demands of both your top talents' individuals and the group in this way. A mentorship program that pairs your best talent with your senior executives is something else you might want to think about. Programs for mentoring may be a very effective tool for developing your present and future leadership when they are well-designed. Because both the mentor and the mentee may grow personally via the mentoring connection, this could be advantageous for your organisation. You might wonder, how? In most of the companies where I worked, the present leadership was older and had more professional experience than your developing leadership or top talents, so I'll generalise here.

For two-way learning, this may provide a great dynamic. Most of the mentors for present leaders have more business knowledge and expertise than your top talent, who may become your future leaders. These seasoned leaders might provide your top people with sound advice on how to advance personally as leaders. However, the majority of your top personnel were digital natives who could show your seasoned leaders different approaches to functioning through the use of cutting-edge technologies.

In the end, the organisation was the biggest winner because it had leaders who were more computer-savvy and talented and those who were more business-aware—a process called "reverse mentoring." I've provided you with some excellent advice on how to consider and organize the growth of your best employees by enabling them to develop and offering them the freedom to accept new challenges, and in the process, creating a community of future leaders. Now it's your chance to use your imagination and consider how you may apply these strategies to the top talent program at your organisation

Imagine that you are the CEO of a global corporation. And four of the most important roles in the organisation became vacant within a six-month period. An external headhunter often needs several months to fill a senior executive level vacancy.And it will take the individual a few more months to become proficient in their new function and get up to speed. What effect do you believe the absence of the ideal candidate for a crucial position would have on your organisation? It may be disastrous. This was the actual situation at the business when I put a top talent program in place.

How to manage a talent database?

It's time to prioritise talent data and look past these constraints. It is anticipated that the post-pandemic boom will alter how organisations have functioned. For instance, to ensure a lean staff aboard, crew member roles are being redesigned in the maritime sector. Technological solutions will unavoidably be used in order to automate and remotely operate ships as much as possible. A talent database that includes primary, secondary, and additional breakdowns of skills for marine engineers and crew members employed by a shipping organisation will be invaluable in this situation for enabling informed decision-making regarding additional training and role reimagination.

Having complete, accurate, and up-to-date talent data that is derived from the following essential inputs may help save training costs, improve employee experience (EX), stop talent flight, and prevent needless hiring costs: Collecting and recording such data should become easier and more pleasant using AI and automation solutions, such as straightforward employee experience bots, as opposed to utilising clumsy forms and substantial Excel tools. A significant amount of organic data may emerge through communication and collaboration technologies, depending on where an organisation is on its path to becoming a contemporary, connected workplace.

With excellent intentions and a distinct vision, they should receive equivalent treatment at work. Although this must be carried out with organisation-specific subtleties, the following general considerations may be taken into account: If there is a flexible career progression, millennials are eager to present and implement new ideas.Therefore, it justifies some fast-tracking and the performance management system can establish a healthy differentiation without discriminating.

Businesses should be prepared to re-evaluate job descriptions and remuneration on a regular basis in light of changing conditions.Some of the current occupations can be divided, grouped together, or rearranged. Literature on job design might be useful in this regard. Additionally, relying primarily on benchmarking to determine remuneration may not be a good idea. Millennials prefer "partnerships" with their employers over more traditional transactional relationships.They anticipate that their growth will be entwined with that of their organisation. The latter ought to guarantee the professional growth of its young workers by giving them access to learning opportunities with increased PL-ownership, freedom to work for a brief period of time in diverse fields, significant L&D programmes, etc. This originally referred to the physical aspect of matching infrastructure but has now devolved into a hygiene concern. Businesses should invest in maintaining a suitable internal infrastructure for health and wellbeing.

Online tests that determine cognitive, behavioural, and skill levels are also very helpful during the employment process. To have a meaningful conversation with millennials, it's critical to help them visualise themselves in the appropriate position at the appropriate location. A millennial's decision to accept an offer is based on more than simply the salary or the reputation of the organisation. A purpose other than profit and success, how the employer brand aligns with their own personal brand, flexible work hours, online collaboration tools at work, benefits aligned with their social needs, value in what they would be doing, demonstrating that you genuinely care about them, and the overall work environment are all critical factors in attracting the right set of millennial talent.

Finally, there should be adequate space for entertaining activities . The aforementioned criteria may, of course, be modified to some extent while maintaining the fundamental idea, depending on things like the nature of the profession, financial feasibility, etc. However, both in the short and long terms, the total effect is most likely to be favourable. This infusion of youth will be heard and visible throughout the whole organisation if the right infrastructure is in place.

How to build a best employees rewarding platform?

Rewards and adoration should be included in expressions of appreciation. Praise for millennials' work in public venues helps them feel that their job has a bigger purpose, which improves their mood. Furthermore, what works for the majority of them is giving them time off to be their creative selves, to think outside of their daily chores, and to come up with something special. Millennials advocate for balancing personal and corporate goals and actively change what is required for a positive organisational culture. In addition, they are more likely than Boomers to have a full-time working spouse or partner, making it harder for them to balance work and family in the previous five years. Many of them are also carers for children and elderly parents.

"Why not see what happens when you challenge your employees to bring all of their talents to their job and reward them not for doing it just like everyone else, but for pushing the envelope, being adventurous, creative, and open-minded, and trying new things?" – Tony Hsieh, former Zappos CEO

For this generation, work-life balance or integration is crucial. Do not mistake their need for balance with "millennial sloth" or a bad work attitude. They don't seek strict separations between their lives and their jobs. They only want to be able to work more freely and evaluate themselves based on production rather than the amount of time they spend hooked into time-tracking software.

The organisational rewards good and low performance through bonuses, incentive pay, and substantive pay differences, according to the compensation viewpoint. This is a beginning step in the direction of depending on human capital as a source of competitive advantage, but it falls short of fully utilising HR as a strategic asset.

Create an atmosphere of reward. Your employees will be more motivated to succeed if they consistently feel like they are scoring goals. In reality, several studies have revealed a strong relationship between positive reinforcement and worker performance. According to the American Psychological Association, providing employees with recognition, awards, and reinforcement has a direct impact on their motivation levels, engagement, productivity, and retention. Congratulate a person for completing a task on time. Show your appreciation for late nights by giving up one. In addition to boosting your employee's self-confidence, rewarding positive behaviour can also increase motivation and productivity.

It has never been more important to provide a variety of services that support millennials' social, physical, mental, and emotional well-being. Since more millennials than any other generation report having depression, there needs to be a special emphasis on mental wellbeing. If millennials perceive the benefit in the value that they generate, they will work harder, quicker, and better as opposed to not being clear about what they are doing and how it will affect the organisation. Counseling, mindfulness practises, and peer support groups are very helpful in this endeavour. This generation is strongly motivated by profit-sharing, monetary prizes, stronger incentives tied to performance or goals, and friendly rivalry. The propensity of millennials to transfer careers, try various positions within an organisation, and change employment says volumes about their openness to experimentation and taking chances. They cannot survive in a society that penalises mistakes made when taking calculated risks. Organisations must embrace "intrapreneurship" rather than discourage it, offer millennials the freedom to experiment, and give as much weight to a good idea coming from a highly experienced individual at the top.

What you need to know about the HR Performance Management System?

Management successfully conveys to employees what is expected of them to perform their tasks efficiently through consistent feedback and reviews. It enables workforces to identify areas of inefficiency, close those loopholes, and produce positive results. CPM helps to create flexible work environments and gives employees the tools they need to be as productive as possible.Modern management is quickly realising this. Performance reviews that are part of annual reviews are quickly losing their relevance. Organisations are being forced to reconsider the feasibility of traditional performance-based management systems as a result of the growing engagement of young workers, particularly those from the millennial generation and Gen-Z. The majority of this new generation of workers are ambitious people who detest status quo circumstances, desire meaningful relationships with their bosses and subordinates, and always strive to learn new things.

The new generation of workers likes to receive feedback on their work performance continuously and in real-time rather than receiving annual or semi-annual evaluations that may appear retroactive, stiff, and out of context. Performance management, in contrast to performance evaluation, is a prospective process that adopts a comprehensive strategy for evaluating employee performance. The Performance Management approach fosters participation among managers and employees while establishing workplace goals and targets. They are urged to evaluate employees' performance collectively, determine if they are improving or regressing, and then create learning and development plans to assist them in upskilling and looking for new opportunities for advancement in their fields of employment.

Performance management, when used in the proper way, can remove tension and toxic behaviour from workplaces where employees are not afraid to confront their bosses with difficult questions. Employers and employees will be in a better position to collaborate in order to see crises in the making and jointly snuff them out by implementing course correction measures. By providing the necessary tools and resources to continuously assess and monitor employee behaviour, performance management must play a crucial role in human resource management (HRM).

Performance measurement is a measure of how well or poorly a person performs in their current or previous positions. It is generally simple to recognize since it can be seen. Target attainment, the what, and, in many businesses today, the how, or the behaviors one utilises to achieve the objectives, are all included in measurements. As part of an organisation's performance management process, these are often evaluated once or twice a year during an employee's mid-or end-of-year review.

On a scale of three to five, performance is often graded using the following descriptors: doesn't meet expectations; completely meets expectations; and surpasses expectations. Potential, on the other hand, relates to how much potential an employee has to grow, develop, and take on a greater or broader position in the future and is harder to evaluate because it isn't as immediately visible and predictable as performance.

Many organisations have started to eliminate employees because of the proposed linkages between yearly performance reviews and employee disengagement. Yet, in many cases, this has also halted the relevant feedback that is essential to employee engagement. There is no "best practise" in this situation; the key is to strike a balance and acknowledge that a strategy that could work for one organisation might not work for another.

Understanding the performance process's goal and developing a proper strategy are the ways to get the ideal balance of productivity and engagement. Organisations should try to rethink performance management such that constant feedback, acknowledgment, and development become the guiding principles rather than do away with performance evaluations altogether.

People frequently discuss whether or not someone has realised their full potential. However, they frequently make quite arbitrary judgments. I've used a three-step strategy to handle issues in talent programs. You can't overcommunicate with ideas like these. Second, I encourage people making nominations for the Top Talent Program to provide instances of particular categories of potential, and I provide examples to help them understand. Let's assume you believe your top talents have the potential to be very strong in learning agility.

Simply said, the basic goal of performance management is to increase organisational performance by assisting teams and individuals to become more productive. It is crucial to maximising employees' potential and elevating their worth to the organisation as assets and valued resources. By encouraging the development of a collaborative culture inside the organisation, CPM will aid in maximising the efficiency and competence of all workers, encourage the exchange of best work practises across remote workforces, and provide Indian businesses with a distinct competitive advantage.

Given the scarcity of talent on the other side of the world, maintaining the business culture should continue to be one of the top concerns for organisations as workers continue to work remotely. You've all put forth a lot of effort to foster a work environment where employees are encouraged to participate, remain productive, and find joy and fulfilment in their jobs. And even if remote work clearly has the potential to become the norm from which you are unlikely to backtrack, it need not interfere with any of that.

Although they can contribute, even electronically, team-building exercises and other business-related outings, celebrations, and events are not the foundation of a's culture. Teams need to feel connected and fulfilled in the virtual environment that employers must develop. Teams must maintain the enchantment you "feel" while seated next to your coworkers, when every voice is heard and every contribution is valued, despite being forced behind screens. Constant contact with management and coworkers seems to be one of the requirements for this.

Have you ever taken a test that measures your capacity to reason logically through challenging problems?

So this is how setting up your talent assessment meetings goes. But don't worry; this script will go over all you need to know so that you'll be ready. Make sure you have the correct individuals in the room who can effectively analyse and calibrate similar talents and have fruitful discussions because all the nominated managers must participate in order to exhibit their talents. This may be chopped in a variety of ways. Level, functional area, geography, performance, or prospective ratings might all be used.

The organisation rationale should go through a few versions before being presented to some of your key stakeholders for comment. In most situations, you would provide two or three versions before sharing the various choices with a few chosen business and human resources leaders to elicit their opinion. If you ask important individuals to express their ideas, it will be much simpler to gain support for and validation of your plans. They may have insights or viewpoints that you don't have from your vantage point, so it's a good idea to give their advice some thought even if you don't necessarily have to heed it. There were very distinct functional and geographic boundaries in one business where I implemented the top talent program.

In its study on the implications of COVID-19 on the workplace, HR consultancy firm Mercer found that more than 40% of businesses saw a moderate to high impact on how their network managed the cultural and organisational change to working online. It is naturally challenging to create a positive working environment across all industries and regions while working remotely without sufficient face-to-face contacts. This may be particularly difficult in developing and rising industries like blockchain, ed-tech, etc. that continue to draw significant numbers of young professionals who are just starting their careers.

How to identify, develop, and retain your High Potential Talent?

Since there is a leadership skills shortage in over 80% of Indian enterprises, HIPO programs are becoming more and more popular. Impacts include a lack of competent leaders; leaders who don't match corporate demands; and crucial positions that go unfilled because aspiring leaders aren't prepared. The majority of organisations anticipate that more than 40% of today's leadership jobs will look quite different in five years, which is another factor contributing to their appeal. HIPO employees are 91% more valuable to an organisation than non-HIPO employees. By just adding a star, these chosen individuals may increase the standard for other employees' performance. A performer alone increases the effectiveness of the other team members by 5% to 15%.

According to Capterra research, most companies don't do enough to teach their new managers; 40% of managers claim to have had less than two hours of management training. Effective management is very crucial for your organisation. Good managers may raise productivity by as much as 50%, while failing managers can increase turnover by 60%! Two hours of training is not enough for one of the most important jobs in an organisation. For new managers, the move from peer to leader can be challenging, but online learning solutions can help by offering continuous training resources that significantly improve managers' performance. All the topics a new manager needs to be successful are covered by microlearning , and with these quick, interactive films, your staff can learn while still completing the regular activities that keep your organisation running.

However, a lot of companies have trouble finding, nurturing, and keeping high-potential employees in their ranks. These individuals are the most competent, driven, and likely to advance to positions of authority within the organisation. Companies frequently use formal high-potential programs to aid these individuals, prepare them for future leadership roles in a disciplined way, and nurture their talent.

However, relatively few businesses appear to be certain that their High Potential program is effective and yielding results. According to a Gartner analysis, the great majority of HiPo initiatives are failing. According to research, only around 15% of participants in HIPO programs have the capacity to lead teams and the organisation as a whole.

Managing HIPO's is usually difficult. They are hard to work with, self-centered, and unyielding in their demands. If the HIPO programs they are participating in do not challenge them and live up to their expectations, they will stop wasting their time. They will hunt for employment chances with other companies that, in their opinion, will more accurately assess their qualifications. Without the proper HIPO program in place, you could be wasting your time and actively driving your best employees away.

HIPOs, which should not be confused with "high-performing" workers, stand out because they represent "high potential," which is the capacity to take on a wider range of duties or to perform the essential duties of leadership. According to the research, an organisation may greatly benefit frmm having these high-potential employees. Some people are either more inherently talented in a certain field or have the capacity to become more skilled in that area. Let's demonstrate this using a sports metaphor. Why do professional sports organisations have a complex selection, evaluation, recruitment, and development procedure for elite athletes? Simple. Considering that these elite athletes have the capacity to inspire their teams to success, bring in sponsors and fans, and earn millions of dollars, that is the reason. In the business world, nothing has changed.

Can you identify your High-potential employees?

It's a rather straightforward solution. These are individuals who have the capacity to significantly increase your organisation's tangible worth. Top talent is sometimes interchanged with high potential in business. A recent Gartner study found that high-potential employees are 91% more valuable to their employers than their colleagues. The development of essential skills and competences will be HR leaders' top priority in 2022, according to the recent Gartner poll. Currently, among the top five concerns for HR executives for the upcoming year are diversity, equity, and inclusion. In a survey conducted by Gartner, Inc., more than 60% of HR leaders responded that in 2022, building critical skills and competencies will be their top priority. A study of more than 550 HR leaders conducted in July 2021 found that diversity, equality, and inclusion (DEI) (35%), present and future leadership bench (45%), organisational design and change management (48%), and the future of work (42%) are the other top HR objectives for 2022.

HR leaders may keep tabs on developments in HIPO identification, talent evaluations, succession planning, and the efficacy and diversity of these programmes by using this report and the associated slides. More than 40% of current leadership jobs, according to the majority of businesses, will appear quite different in five years. As a result, companies are investing in high-potential employee initiatives, with 65% doing so at the expense of other personnel costs. Global learning and development leaders are surveyed by Gartner every year to learn more about HIPO development goals, program implementation, and effectiveness. Compare your HIPO development initiatives to global norms to make tactical adjustments that improve performance.

Using Gartner's HIPO Competency Prioritisation Guide, identify the business-driven abilities that top performers and future leaders in your organisation must have. Evaluate the organisational demands of the present and future and specify the abilities that will be used to assess HIPO applicants. It is impossible to exaggerate how crucial it is to keep high-potential employees (HIPOs), and the conventional method is no longer sufficient.

How to nurture and retain your HIPO talent in a hybrid work environment?

The use of hybrid designs has proven to be a crucial improvement. According to surveys, more than 77% of workers would prefer to keep working remotely, and 30% would completely resign if required to do so. However, it is impossible to discount the advantages of office settings and face-to-face collaboration. As a result of the excessive use of video conferencing during the epidemic, digital tiredness has become widespread. As a result, a hybrid model approach could prove to be the perfect balancing act.

In addition to the primary objective of attaining flexible work hours, there are various benefits to establishing a hybrid workspace model for the organisation and employees. In the near term, a hybrid strategy gives businesses the chance to continue operating and making money while managing the unpredictable nature of the pandemic. Long-term, it offers flexibility to individuals who either need it or desire it. Additional benefits of the hybrid work paradigm include cost savings from leasing fewer office spaces as well as time and money saved on commuting and transportation. Additionally, it gives access to a larger pool of local and international talent, drawing and keeping competent and varied workforces from a variety of geographical locations.

Initiatives for employee contentment in a hybrid workplace must include both remote and regular office workers. Failure to incorporate hybrid teams and remote workers into your contentment efforts might result in failure to interact with the majority of your team members for businesses that are totally remote or have a significant percentage of employees that work flexible schedules. Engage remote workers by addressing both their individual and team contentment requirements. Start by conducting a poll of your employees to determine their current levels of involvement and any preferred means by which you might help them increase those levels. The most considerate approach to interacting with employees is frequently the simplest.

You'll not only get the answers you need when you start this process by directly asking your team members what your organisation can do to help them connect more deeply with their job, but you'll also be sending a message to your employees that their wellbeing is your top priority. You may then go ahead and develop employee contentment activities that put the wellness of your remote employees first, using your employee feedback as a springboard, like: allowing for hybrid and flexible scheduling. Allowing employees to work from home, they claim, would make 77% of them happier. If you want your remote and hybrid employees to be engaged in their jobs, you should review your corporate culture and make sure they feel included in the overall goals of the organisation.

How would you look at both sides of the coin?

A suitable remote work culture is also advantageous for your business when the staff is required to return to the office and fully embrace on-site work. A vibrant teleworking culture is, after all, just that. Better connections, more trust, and improved communication are a few of the wonderful effects when the team links of remote employees are reinforced. It facilitates communication and collaboration between remote workers and their office peers and helps the change from remote to office work go more easily. All of these elements work together to assist a business in retaining personnel and establishing an effective workflow.

Enhancing end-user experience and achieving corporate objectives at a reasonable cost are the main goals of digital transformation. Inclusion, collaboration, transparency, and security are the four main pillars of hybrid workplaces. Only with the aid of technology is the aforementioned accomplishment achievable. The future prosperity of every organisation depends on its capacity to harness technology and foster employee digital proficiency. According to McKinsey, bright people want three things in particular: outstanding leaders who will empower them; an organisation with a strong culture; and a job that makes a difference. Then, in order to keep high-potential personnel, it is essential to concentrate on improving the three areas described above rather than making unrealistic promises.

If you intend to hire remote workers, make sure to set up three crucial support pillars for them: There is nothing worse than joining a new team and feeling like you have to ask questions all the time in order to understand things. You can help your remote workers integrate successfully and successfully into your organisation (both culturally and professionally!) by giving them the required training materials and organisation knowledge. An extensive and well-structured information base After the first onboarding, it is crucial to have an organisation-wide resource dump with all the data your workers require to succeed on your team.

On the other hand, loneliness is an issue that remote workers face more and more. People may come together and share a shared objective when there is a consistently positive remote work culture. Additionally, it promotes a sense of belonging and inspires practical actions like impromptu check-ins and informal conversations that end distant isolation. Gaining top management commitment to act on survey data and neglecting to employ focus groups to dive into the source of issues are common mistakes organisations make with contentment surveys. In the majority of cases (72%), employees want more responsibility in their jobs. Additionally, people are more likely to be committed to and interested in their job when they are given the responsibilities they desire. This means that managers should take the time to get to know their employees and offer them as much responsibility as they desire (and can reasonably handle). An employee who has too little duty or too much responsibility will perform poorly.

The ability to maintain a healthy work-life balance, on the other hand, invariably results in higher levels of job satisfaction and better emotional involvement. Hybrid workplaces have some drawbacks, including less teamwork and communication, a higher risk of cybersecurity breaches, and a silo effect between office and remote workers. Fortunately, using technology wisely allows us to get over these obstacles and maximise the benefits of the hybrid approach.

The environment for remote work is always changing. Even while each difficulty may be discussed in detail, embracing them as necessary for the moment might help define the new normal. Building trust and allowing for transparency makes it possible to retain the finest personnel despite the genuine challenge of sustaining a good remote work culture. Organisations that are embracing the remote work trend must create a culture that can encourage openness and productivity while also giving workers a feeling of community, even if they are distributed around the globe and seldom ever interact with their coworkers.

What exactly is a culture of remote work?

The notion that remote employees may not be taken into account for promotions or chances to lead projects is something that may be increasingly common for hybrid teams. When it comes to promotions, it is easy to assume that remote workers are overlooked when management is in the office and only paying attention to the employees physically seated around them.

Businesses are prepared to resume operations in a safe and gradual way as vaccination rates throughout the world rise and the reopening of workplaces is imminent. Organisations have continued to develop methods of operations utilising digital technology platforms after observing India slide in and out of many lockdowns over the previous 18 months.

Through a focus on the employee experience and the development of flexible, digital, and secure work models, organisations' attention has gradually switched to the seamless integration of work, workplace, and workforce.

It would seem rational for businesses to foster a diverse workforce while still taking into account the preferences of each employee. The hybrid workplace approach creates an efficient combination of in-person and online workspaces. It offers a way to strike a balance between each employee's demands and preferences on the one hand, and their capacity for cooperation and productivity in a common "physical" area on the other.

The remote work culture, to put it simply, is a set of values and methods that extends outside the walls of a regular workplace. No matter where they are located, it links each employee to the organisation. Good remote work cultures foster a sense of community among employees that transcends geographical limitations. Every employee, after all, intuitively knows what is expected of them, when they may operate autonomously, and what acts are valued. It is even more crucial for organisations to think about creating a sustainable remote work culture and putting related technologies and procedures in place in order to allow all of this for a growing remote workforce. You should think about how you can consistently connect with your team, especially your remote employees, and promote productivity and growth without isolating or micromanaging them in order to keep them motivated. Here are several suggestions that, regardless of where employees are located, have been shown to effectively bind teams together.

- Start at the top by encouraging your team leaders to develop stronger relationships with their teams or enlisting them in leadership programs; employee contentment varies by 70% depending on how well-connected they are to their managers.

- All workers should have growth opportunities available to them, such as frequent one-on-one meetings when employees may discuss their individual objectives and the particular methods in which your business can assist them in achieving those goals.

- Create an education assistance program to demonstrate to employees your commitment to their involvement; 94% of employees believe they would be more likely to stay at an organisation longer if they believed the organisation was committed to their professional growth.

- Showing workers the immediate outcomes of their work will help them to connect with their job on a deeper level since they will be able to clearly see how important each employee's contributions are to the business.

- It takes a lot of time and effort to develop a positive remote work culture where teams feel trusted and motivated to perform at their highest level. But if you want to keep elite talent, it's also one of the easy picks.

- You must be ready with all of the best practises and resources to ensure that your workers have a smooth transition, whether you are launching a new remote team or converting your entire organisation to remote work.

- The goal is to create a culture that fosters openness, creates a climate of trust, and serves as a role model for other organisations.

- Open up the opportunity for employees in the office and those who work remotely to "apply" for new positions or large projects that need a leader; everyone must have a fair chance.

- You may try making a separate project that is only accessible to the remote crew to take it a step further.

- Utilising these strategies will improve the working environment for your remote team while also enhancing your corporate culture.
- Making the effort to keep your remote workers interested in your business can help them feel really connected to it and inspired to perform their best job.
- Regardless of how you go about it, giving every person in the organisation a chance to take on leadership responsibilities is a terrific way to maintain morale. Big and small tasks are both possible. The challenge will always have a willing participant.
- When a remote team member sees "office happy hour" on the corporate calendar, they are aware that they will be missing out on the social interaction amongst coworkers during that time.
- Survey data says that when working remotely, employees miss out on social interactions and celebrations the most.
- Your organisation may also take team gatherings into account when planning their yearly or quarterly meeting schedule.
- Bring the remote team in, but don't simply leave it there. When everyone is there, this is a fantastic opportunity to foster genuine fellowship.
- You should make the following plans: a celebration or an after-hours corporate function. Your attention should be directed towards group activities that promote cooperation and joint work.
- A weekly video chat is one of the best ways to stay in touch with your remote team on a regular basis. While some remote workers would rather send a short email or Slack chat, others yearn for in-person communication. It fosters interest and connection on

a new level. Phone and video calls also take into consideration tone and reduce the likelihood of misunderstandings. 93% of workers agree that video communication makes distant workers feel more connected.

- If you've ever collaborated with remote workers, you'll probably recall that your communication style didn't particularly differ from that of your other team members. There are several ways to instantly connect with others in our modern environment. Your remote team is just a few clicks away from Slack and email. The larger emphasis will be on keeping in regular contact with team members that you may not connect with frequently since you don't see them five days a week.

How Learning and Development can impact your organisation?

Learning and development are ranked as the most significant job perk by 42% of employees. More than any other intangible benefit, chances for professional growth and advancement are desired by nearly half of your workforce. Additionally, it's likely that those who prioritise upward mobility are also high achievers and ambitious. Retaining your most valued team members depends greatly on providing them with a route for advancement. But keep in mind that a sizable portion of individuals also choose to stay where they are and carry on doing what they are already doing. The corporation values these workers as well. A person who has held the same position for a long time is a great resource for assisting with new team member training and enhancing productivity throughout that tier of the business. Making growth opportunities available to people who desire them is the best strategy in this situation. However, don't discipline employees who fail to utilize the resources for advancement.

Recently, the learning paradigm changed from a "supervising" pattern to one that emphasises "collaboration" and "mentoring." It indicates that leading businesses have begun implementing a peer-to-peer learning strategy. Such a strategy encourages peer mentoring and training, not that of outside consultants or supervisors. Peer-to-peer learning offers a number of noteworthy benefits.

When learning with others, people first feel less anxious about making mistakes or failing. Second, peer-to-peer training supports greater decision-making, employee empowerment, and self-governance inside organisations. Finally, it enables the expansion of information exchange and expertise inside a business. A common feature of contemporary skill management platforms is the mentoring-matching feature, which encourages bottom-up learning and makes peer-to-peer learning more open, creative, and transparent. The matching system links workers, highlighting mentors who could be a good fit.

It's imperative that you set your HIPO programme apart from your more general L&D activities in order to effectively serve your high-potential personnel. All of your employees should have access to training materials and development opportunities, but your HIPO efforts will be concentrated on progressing individuals in your workforce who have the potential to be leaders. You may use the following recommended practises to ensure that your HIPOs reach their maximum potential:

- Align the development of high-potential employees with strategic objectives.

- Where you want to position your HIPOs and how they get there will ultimately depend on your overall organisation objectives.
- The need for and availability of leadership roles is determined by the organisation's growth, thus your HIPOs development has to be planned to support business acceleration.
- To achieve this successfully, it's imperative to ensure that your HiPo programme has support and buy-in at the C-staff level.
- Planning for the future and swiftly filling open positions as they arise is also made possible by preparing your HIPOs for leadership responsibilities before such jobs are formally formed. In a similar vein, this enables you to consistently add HIPO's prospects to your leadership pipeline.
- It takes a team to choose applicants for your HIPO programme.
- Make certain that your recruiting managers and other departmental executives are aware of the standards previously outlined.
- They are required to keep an eye out for HIPOs and give suggestions for their growth and development as part of their work duties.
- The most effective opportunity to provide feedback, discuss goal-setting, evaluate performance, and assess development potential is often during routine check-ins with direct reports.
- If high potential has been identified, your supervisors can recommend their direct reports for the HIPO development program.
- Give HIPO employees measurable career objectives and acknowledgement.

- Give your HIPO staff what they desire.

A common feature of contemporary skill management platforms is the mentoring-matching feature, which encourages bottom-up learning and makes peer-to-peer learning more open, creative, and transparent. The matching system links workers, highlighting mentors who could be a good fit. The workers can better help one another in certain projects or tasks by doing this.The mentorship programme JetBlue Scholars, run by the American airline JetBlue, is a striking illustration of peer-to-peer learning. In this programme, more experienced coworkers train and advise junior coworkers who lack a college degree. The organisation was able to decrease tuition costs by around $2.8 million as a consequence, and employee happiness rose to an impressive 85%. You understand that HIPO workers are crucial to the development and success of the organisation as a people leader. Many top companies launch learning and development programs that are designed to help these particular team members in an effort to engage and keep HIPO employees. Let's discuss how you can help your HIPO employee program achieve its full potential as well, from methods for locating HIPO personnel to professional advice on how to develop a new programme or revamp an existing one.

"Despite substantial efforts by HR and learning professionals, a multibillion dollar leadership development industry, and more than 70 years of leadership research, organisations' overall success at growing leaders remains dismal."- Deloitte High Impact Leadership Survey Report

If you know what to look for, it's easy to spot those HIPOs that already provide results for you. On the basis of the following standards, you may identify the HIPOs in your organisation:

- Instead of focusing only on their own accomplishments, they are interested in the performance and success of the entire team. They are creative, adaptable learners who smoothly incorporate new knowledge and methods into their work.
- They are interested in both their own professional progress and the expansion of the organisation, and they want to advance their talents in both areas.
- They are aware of the impact their position has on their team members, their division, and the business as a whole.
- They are capable and demonstrate skill in their job, but they also seek perfection and graciously take criticism.
- Candidates for new HIPO recruitment should exhibit many of the same traits as your current HIPO staff. You can determine this through interviews and a review of their employment history.
- You must learn how to develop your program using objective criteria, a communication strategy that controls expectations, and a precise, quantifiable description of performance and potential that appeals to your stakeholders.
- You must learn how to gather the correct data, organize it in a useful way that facilitates decision-making, and present it to perform nomination, calibration, and selection processes efficiently.
- You must learn strategies and best practises for growing, using, and renewing your talent pool; placing your high potential in positions and tasks that are crucial to the success of your business; and more. They may all be

excellent at what they do, but it's crucial to note that HIPOs demonstrate managerial skills that not all of your top staff may possess.

Why is "employees' happiness" so important?

- According to Gartner Research's 2021 HIPO and Succession Management Benchmarking Report, to achieve your organisational main goals, you must successfully discover and promote diverse, high-potential people.
- According to a thorough study on happiness and productivity, happy employees produce 13% more. When it comes to employee productivity, employers may want to take note of how crucial a pleasant mental state may be to their benefit.
- The research also tracked the relationship between employee performance and happiness. Results showed a relationship between a bad working culture and lower levels of production and happiness.
- Employers who desire a successful wellness program should keep in mind that employee satisfaction can improve general health and lower medical expenses. Happier individuals experience lower overall mortality rates, quicker healing from accidents and illnesses, and a lower risk of diseases like diabetes and stroke, according to research that linked physical health with happiness.
- The happy employee offers advice on fostering respect, winning trust, and exercising leadership based on research and years of professional experience. By using appropriate communication strategies and powerful incentives, you'll discover how to create and keep high-performance teams.

- Every employee counts now more than ever because of shrinking workforces, hiring freezes, and productivity challenges. The Happy employee will assist you in locating and hiring the most brilliant staff, keeping them on board, and ensuring their happiness and productivity.

- According to the study, 68% of US workers still seek the convenience of working from home. If they are not given the option of remote work, some employees may even consider changing jobs. The data demonstrates how reluctant employees are to resume their regular work environments.

- Employees who are satisfied with their work stay in their positions four times longer than those who are not, spend twice as much time on assignments, and have 65% more energy.

- Improved mood and emotional well-being are closely associated with physical activity and a nutritious diet. A positive outlook supports employees in continuing to make healthy decisions in all areas of their lives, in addition to happiness producing these habits.

"Happy workers amount to better productivity, better motivation, and a better organisation culture."

Measurements of HR's impact on the success of the organisation mirrored this perspective. Theorists specifically looked at techniques and practises that are concentrated at the level of the individual worker, job, and practise (such as employee selection, incentive compensation, and so forth). The notion was that if individual employee performance improved, it would inevitably boost organisational performance as well.

Despite attempts to broaden the scope of HR's effect, such research accomplished nothing to establish HR as a new source of competitive advantage. The difficulties of a strategic HR architecture were only dimly seen. Simply put, it didn't inspire HR managers to reevaluate their position. The organisation pays employees and recruits individuals, but it doesn't prioritise finding the top candidates or nurturing unique talent.

What are those things to ponder about Human resource Management?

- Make sure employees put their theoretical knowledge into practise by approaching routine activities in novel ways in order to help them reach their full potential as employees.
- Celebrate even the smallest successes and stress each employee's contribution to the organisation's success.
- Undoubtedly, there is a connection between employee engagement and training. Therefore, it is the responsibility of HR and senior management to encourage a culture of learning, make the learning process accessible, and encourage team building among employees.
- The epidemic compelled businesses to adopt remote working in the vast majority of situations. Nowadays, companies are not afraid to experiment with novel resourcing strategies. If freelancers and gig workers are accepted, traditional HR information systems that are ill-equipped to manage employee talent data would come to a grinding halt. And this strengthens the case for businesses to think about implementing sophisticated talent information systems and taking delight in actually understanding their employees.

- A member of the product team could know that they are performing well, but they might desire to learn more about marketing. To establish that united accountability, a shared solution and space are essential.
- Creating a space where you can talk about your goals and how you're doing at meeting them could benefit your entire organisation.
- Shared objectives help with responsibility and focus, and they also give you the advantage of knowing what everyone is working on, wherever they are in the world.
- Having access to cross-organisation goals will also make them feel like a member of the bigger team.
- Salary and job descriptions, however, are only the beginning of the process of building a contented, motivated workforce.
- Employees that are engaged show interest and commitment in their work. And developing connections is more important than having fair pay rates for employees if you want to get them motivated and invested in their work.
- In the modern world, when dispersed teams and remote workers are common, this is even more true. You've gathered some of our top employee happiness ideas for both in-person and remote teams to assist you in creating your own contented workforce.
- Every employee has to be aware of the common objective and how they may each contribute, both individually and collectively, to moving the business in that direction. This one starts at the very top.
- The organisation must have a clear grasp of its goals and values and convey them to all levels of personnel.
- Employee happiness and productivity are likely to increase when awareness and alignment are in place.

- To obtain the happiness you want, you can't just tell everyone how they fit into the organisation and what they need to accomplish.
- Keep in mind that workers must be involved in and enthusiastic about their work.
- Millennials are the backbone of the global workforce, transforming the labour demographics and being a priceless resource for every organisation.
- An organisation need not be a non-profit or social enterprise to foster an environment where millennial employees feel their job matters.
- Even for HR specialists entrusted with enhancing it, the word "employee happiness" may be hazy.
- The fact that businesses and employees have diverse perspectives on employee happiness makes it challenging to comprehend.
- Employee happiness, to an organisation or management, refers to people's attention to detail and productivity.
- An employee who is engaged in their work is someone who is invested in it. In theory, these two definitions should agree. Because they are involved in and interested in their work, employees pay attention and produce more. And everybody is content.
- Giving workers a sense of security and trust will make them feel more at ease carrying out their daily tasks and more capable of succeeding.
- It takes work to create a workplace culture where people feel happy and eager to begin each day. It will need patience and a great deal of effort. But in the long run, it will be worth it tenfold in fresh perspectives, originality, and top-notch work.
- High-potential employees must be retained. Therefore, managers have the authority and obligation to design

programs and take appropriate action.

- At first glance, one could assume that talented workers need excellent rewards, such as a greater income or more perks, in order to be happy in their positions.
- It's important to keep in mind that the three keys to fostering workplace happiness are employee motivation, talent retention, and change management.
- The productivity of a workplace will rise as a result of happiness. People are more devoted to an organisation when they work in a positive and fulfilling atmosphere. In other words, they will offer everything they have and are unlikely to defect from the organisation.
- That much has long been obvious to industry professionals and those in charge, but the issue is virtually always how to effortlessly develop a mutual degree of trust and understanding.
- The trust word is essential to building employee relationships and fostering loyalty. It involves expert comprehension and great balance when building trust, developing an empowered workforce, and, most importantly, letting your people take the lead.
- Despite the fact that Americans made up the study's sample, the results are universal. Because of this, employers must recognize how important it is to build trust with their employees and that this can only happen if they also give their employees room to develop.
- For both employees and employers, trust is a strong basis on which to create a connection that is meaningful, instructive, and mutually profitable. In actuality, this is just a continuation of how relationships in general, whether they be personal or professional, function.
- As a leader, you must actively seek to improve the situation if you believe that the present levels of trust

in the team or organisation are preventing you from reaching your full potential.

- You must raise these issues with your manager as an employee or team member and do your part to maintain a high degree of team trust.

- Employees must comprehend the overarching corporate plan and how it applies to them. They must understand how they can be successful and contribute to the organisation. When things don't match, danger begins.

- Productivity and attention are low. Increased employee turnover Then, high management exerts pressure on managers and HR departments to restart those metrics. The issue grows worse if efforts are made to boost productivity when they need to be used to develop new methods to engage and motivate workers.

- All of your staff will know exactly who to contact with questions if you establish a clear line of communication or organisational chart for your whole business. This can prevent employee isolation or disharmony and save your organisation hours of effort each week. Give everyone the chance to flourish.

- Beyond sight, beyond memory the belief that a person is somehow less a member of the team just because they are not in the office is the largest barrier to remote employee happiness. Due to this negligence, businesses may pass up on highly qualified remote applicants from all over the world.

- Establish contact points for various forms of support: The more time an employee stays with your organisation, the more likely it is that they will cooperate with areas other than their initial job, from the go-to HR person to the major touchpoints on other teams.

- It goes without saying that contented workers perform better. They work harder, provide higher-quality work, and ultimately stay with your business longer.
- People in your organisation wishing to take on a particular project and additional responsibility may find this to be a terrific opportunity.
- Encourage team members in the office and on remote teams to get together and propose a concept to the business because the list of priorities that the leadership is focusing on appears to go on forever. Encourage them to contribute to the improvement of your remote culture.
- Whether they are members of your team or the entire workforce, you must have faith in them. Even if you are not in close proximity to your staff, you should learn to trust them and make sure they have the tools and freedom they need to do their jobs well. This will also be reflected in the daily operations, corporate policies, and programs that the HR department adheres to.
- It's critical for every organisation to keep in touch with its stakeholders on a regular basis. Relationships are strengthened, and HR is made more aware of the state of the workforce. Be precise and straightforward when communicating, and offer feedback frequently.
- It is critical to maintain open lines of communication. In the virtual environment, communication and routine check-ins with team members and employees in general are essential. The communication route chosen is equally significant.
- Use a communication method that is convenient for both parties, such as a phone call, email, or a chat program like MS Teams, Slack, or Google. In the days of physical offices, informal interactions and water cooler

conversations were common.

- Try to create these informal bonds in the modern day by holding virtual coffee dates or other similar get-togethers. As they are absorbed into the culture, HR professionals may take the lead in normalising virtual meet-ups and virtual engagement activities.

- Encourage team leadership skills, especially remote management skills, in individuals in managerial positions.

- Working remotely and coordinating with team members may be key abilities for the majority of employment. Does the applicant feel at ease working in-person, remotely, or both? On the basis of the particular function and the organisational policy, including this in the resume might aid in selecting candidates who are a suitable fit.

- Employees want the freedom, independence, and flexibility to handle their jobs remotely. Top talent shouldn't feel left out or excluded, especially young talent. Micromanagement, on the other hand, is far from the ideal option.

- Of course, technology plays a significant role in the culture of remote work. Nearly 82% of respondents in a survey said workplace technology is a deciding factor when it comes to looking for a new job.

- Actually, millennials are more likely to quit their jobs if they think the technology is substandard. The easiest way to lose top talent is through this.

- The organisation culture in the post-pandemic age should be friendly and uniform for all employees, wherever they work.It should also include a place for objectives and plans that continue to give top people the chance to grow their careers, learn new skills, and broaden their perspectives. All of these opportunities were formerly restricted to office employment, but they now need to relocate to become location independent.

- A leader in a crucial position was departing the organisation once more as you were wrapping up the selecting phase of your program. Because of the program, you were able to fill this important executive job with one of your recently discovered top talents before the current employee departed her post.

- By recognising and nurturing your organisation's future leaders, you will know that you have contributed to its success in the future. Talented and driven individuals now have the chance to grow and realize their full potential. You will influence others through your program.

- In conclusion, nobody can definitively tell you what will make your organisation as contented and healthy as possible. The complexity of the issues we've discussed may seem different in each workplace. But what is certain is that when workers feel appreciated and cared for, they are more likely to respect your leadership and take care of your organisation.

Many companies make a concentrated effort to develop work environments that stimulate personal and professional development, enhance job satisfaction, and motivate workers to find purpose and enjoyment in their work.

"Employees can't be treated as a means to an end. Your organisation's lifeblood is its employees. It will be easier for you to recruit and retain great talent if you put their satisfaction first."- Dr. Amit Das

CHAPTER THREE

Forecast Outcomes With A High Degree Of Certainty

"organisations in the era of competition have no choice but to outperform their rivals in the marketplace. An essential part of supporting the company's strategy plan is human resource management by helping other departments hire the best talent."

Unwanted attrition is an unfortunate but inevitable reality in today's competitive business world. Many business executives throughout the world are living a nightmare that is both eerie and terrible. One of the things that irritates executives the most is when excellent performers abruptly leave and take their talents to another organisation. Initiatives to increase employee engagement are so frequently employed to keep the best. It is still not a foolproof plan, though.

Given that it is difficult to prevent people from leaving, is it feasible to predict attrition so that it only somewhat negatively affects the business? Yes, it is achievable with the aid of predictive analytics and forecasting.

An organisation may determine how many people it will require in the future to achieve its strategic goals by using a technique called human resource forecasting. HR forecasting entails identifying the positions that the business will need to fill, the competencies that candidates must possess to perform those roles, and the difficulties that the business will encounter in trying to fill such positions. Identification and planning for an organisation's evolving people needs now rely heavily on human resource planning.

Although various strategies are used for the benefit of the business and to significantly enhance retention, leaders cannot rely only on them. If they do not maintain an open mind and a realistic stance on the future, they must confront the difficult truth that they will ultimately lose major talent. Influential leaders take proactive measures every day to protect themselves, their teams, and their organisations against the danger of attrition because wishing for retention is not a sound business plan.

Predictive analytics is a crucial step in the analytics journey. It enables businesses to supplement historical data with real-time insights that can subsequently be used to forecast and shape future outcomes. In order to advance business, modern predictive analytics combines machine predictions with human intuition. Foresight is crucial in business. Businesses will be more effective if they can forecast outcomes with a high degree of certainty based on past performance and data points.

It's a prediction algorithm that figures out how vulnerable (or likely) it is for each employee to leave. It informs us, at any given time, of the likelihood that we will lose personnel or a specific employee in the future. Finding out more about the workforce that is now accessible is simply one aspect of the HR forecasting process. organisations must assess their own human resource requirements, which are influenced in part by their size and kind. Many businesses start by gathering information from every department. Utilising different predictive model, it is feasible to identify the employees who are most likely to leave and communicate with them to learn about their concerns.

The organisation's current job positions must be evaluated at the next stage. HR management must consider the types of work performed as well as the number of employees in each class. HR is in charge of assessing employees' present talents after determining what skills and information they need to have to accomplish the organisation's long-term strategic goals.

HR must comprehend the organisation's current and long-term goals in order to accurately estimate manpower needs and so support organisational strategy. Human resources must also plan for the need to change existing roles and create new ones. organisations must enhance their tactics for employees retention and recruiting in light of high employee turnover rates.

Thanks to an unprecedented convergence of intuitive tools, new predictive techniques, and hybrid cloud deployment models, predictive analytics is becoming more accessible to a broader range of society and enabling capabilities for making informed decisions. For those who are unfamiliar, predictive analytics uses data, machine learning methods, and statistical algorithms to make predictions about the future based on the past. It may also be defined as technology that enhances intelligent decision-making abilities by learning from experience.

Predictive analytics, as the name suggests, uses historical data to forecast future events and direct decision-making. For a variety of statistical factors relating to the normal distribution and robustness of particular statistics, forecasts may become more accurate with additional data. To emphasise the idea of this subject, below is an extremely rudimentary illustration:

Probabilistic projections of the future are produced through predictive analytics. Nobody has a crystal ball that is completely accurate. Consider the sport of horse racing. Horses are the subject of wagers based on indicators such as age, pedigree, past performance, etc. The odds are a reflection of all bettors' collective predictions. The favourite at the odds usually prevails and performs as expected. The long shot does, however, occasionally catch everyone off guard.

The idea of predictive analytics is not new. For years, statisticians have used decision trees and regression to assist organisations in correlating, classifying, and forecasting their data. The application of predictive analytics has expanded, which is something new. It is no longer just for statisticians and mathematicians, though. Predictive analytics is becoming more accessible to a wider range of society and is enabling capabilities for making wise judgments thanks to an unparalleled convergence of intuitive tools, new predictive methodologies, and hybrid cloud deployment patterns.

The secret to getting the most out of human capital data is to tie the various data sources to strategic business goals. Utilising data from many sources and applying predictive models together helps to project the right picture and provide a clear, comprehensive analysis of the organisation.

How to utilise human capital with the principles of predictive analytics?

The adoption of analytics that affect people is gaining significant traction at a time when HR is poised for significant transformation, particularly in the post-COVID age. Soon, human capital analytics will be viewed as a key capability. Today's executives understand that their only source of long-term competitive advantage is their workforce. People-related analytics will become more and more in demand. Machines, materials, processes, technology, and information have no effect on their own.

HR managers should focus on whether people are employed in roles that make the best use of their skills, experience, and talents. According to research data, emphasising employee abilities and recognising employees' potential can lead to promotions or other changes in employment duties. Individual work satisfaction is increased, and a organisation's strategic goals are furthered when individuals' abilities are matched to organisational objectives.

What are those popular dynamic forecasting models that can be used?

- The Markov model, a dynamic forecasting model, is now a key quantitative analytic tool in the forecasting of human resources. With the help of this model, HR leaders can accurately predict demand probabilities, the number of potential internal hires and transfers, and the internal supply of human resources that the organisation will have on hand.
- Workload analysis forecasting technique estimates the total projected output of goods and services over a certain time period.

- Using the leaders's opinion method, HR managers evaluate the future manpower requirements for several categories in their individual organisations.
- The HR division finds employees in critical roles using this method and assembles an expert panel. They are asked a series of inquiries on HR requirements. The solutions and suggestions offered by this panel are based on the background knowledge and individual experiences of the panel members.
- The nominal group approach and the Delphi technique are similar but vary in one way. The experts simply need to provide the answer when using the nominal group approach. A facilitator is required by the Delphi approach to gather expert opinions on labour projections.

When humans engage with those items and other people, they produce value. Why would it not be standard corporate practise to use analytics to maximise people's net contributions if they represent 70% of your cost and 100% of your value? Every organisation must have adequate human resources. It is essential to perceive people as assets rather than "costs" to the organisation in the competitive and expanding world of today. With the rapid growth of technology and legislation, skill requirements in a fast-paced environment are always evolving. In order to maintain our competitive advantage and market dominance, we must use analytics to restructure our workforce situations and forecast our best course of action.

Three layers of human capital analytics are described in predictive analytics for human resources:

- To assess links, linkages, correlations, and causations, descriptive analytics looks at past data.
- Predictive analytics forecasts future trends based on historical patterns.
- Prescriptive analytics, which uses complicated data to forecast potential outcomes in order to optimise the workforce, raises the bar for prediction.

Finding key areas where predictive analytics may add value to the HR domain include:

- By effectively segmenting employees, predictive analytics can be used for successful talent management and aid in a better knowledge of the employee base. HR can determine which profiles are more deserved by looking at a statistical relationship between profile elements (such as education and experience) and employee value. This creates long-term benefits for the organisation by significantly lowering recruitment costs and improving quality.
- Predictive learning algorithms can assist in predicting the influence of organisational needs and tailoring the programmes accordingly for superior outcomes. In addition to identifying workers who require particular training, predictive analytics also identifies new trends in a variety of areas, including programme diversity, enrollment, onboarding, employee management, etc.
- By creating focused recruitment strategies, maximising HR partner activities, etc., predictive analytics helps to better estimate the organisational requirements. This makes it possible for businesses to use their resources as efficiently as possible while boosting profitable development.

- To establish or redesign projects for key workers at various levels, HR professionals should take advantage of unstructured and structured data from a variety of sources. In order to obtain insightful and useful input, key employee analysis is more efficient than generic employee surveys. Such data may aid in understanding how different HR initiatives, policies, and organisational changes are viewed by the workforce.

- Predictive analytics enables an organisation to identify employees who are more likely to violate the organisation's security policy, which aids fraud risk management. Employers can create a fraud risk score by utilising statistical modelling approaches to analyse employee activity records. This could perhaps avert financial effects while also preserving the organisation's reputation.

- The HR department tracks the costs associated with various tasks like hiring, training, performance reviews, benefits, incentives, etc. Focusing on the organisation's intangible assets (such as leadership, culture, dedication, and loyalty), HR teams can strengthen their organisational presence while moving in line with strategic objectives.

- Predictive model knowledge may point the way to changes in leadership aptitude, engagement, culture, etc., which can be applied for improved planning and forecasting. Aligning the various data sources to strategic business objectives is the key to getting the most value out of human capital data.

- Utilising data from various sources and applying predictive models aids in projecting the correct image and clarifies a comprehensive study of the organisation. Combining organisational data with statistical data from the government and other sources offers a solid foundation for efficient planning and achieving the organisation's short-and long-term objectives.

HR teams need to go beyond operational analytics to predictive skills in order to play a more strategic role in the organisation. This allows them to contribute more to advancing the strategic organisational vision and objectives. Predictive analytics assists businesses in enhancing exceptional employee experiences that will contribute to the achievement of anticipated long-term goals with the intended maximum efficiency.

How does HR analytics offer a practical approach to using data to solve real HR challenges in organisations?

With clear guidelines and recommendations for creating the business case, launching an HR analytics function, avoiding common pitfalls, presenting data through visualisation and storytelling, and much more, HR Analytics offers a practical approach to using data to solve real HR challenges in organisations.

The development of strategic partnerships goes beyond HR professionals merely defending their position or territory. It has ramifications for the organisation's overall existence. The HR department runs the danger of being outsourced if it can't demonstrate its worth. This isn't always a negative thing in and of itself; exporting ineffective tasks might help improve an organisation's overall bottom line. However, it can waste vital potential.

Do you want your best employees to expand your organisation, lead the organisation through transformation, or develop into excellent people leaders?

More than ever, an organisation's need to prioritise its employees' well-being over other benefits is known as the "wellness imperative." Businesses with engaged employees who have a personal connection to their job should expect increased productivity, lower customer turnover, and better brand recognition among internal and external stakeholders. The bulk of today's workforce worldwide is made up of millennials, who have dramatically changed the makeup of the labour force.

How can you expect potential clients to be enthusiastic about your business if your employees are disengaged and alienated from the work they are doing?

A new employee joins your organisation with enthusiasm, motivation, and plenty of fresh ideas. The passion and energy they had when they first entered the building then gradually diminished as the days grew into months. The effort to maintain employee engagement is continuous for many organisations.

Additionally, disengaged employees may have increased absenteeism rates, lower productivity, higher turnover, more opportunities for human error, safety problems, and other issues.

Don't be alarmed if this sounds familiar. You are not alone either. These same difficulties and obstacles have been faced by several top HR executives, CEOs, and prosperous business owners. However, many of them have also discovered ways to tackle this engagement head on. One of the most significant adjustments you can make to your organisation's bottom line is to focus on increasing employee engagement. According to the study, organisations with engaged teams perform 202% better than those with disengaged teams.

How else can you pinpoint the factors that influence employee engagement in your organisation?

Contrary to what many executives may believe, inspiring employees requires much more than simple pay and benefits. Additionally, it is impossible to generalise about the characteristics that influence involvement because they vary by organisation, generation, and job. According to research, the following factors consistently promote employee engagement across a variety of generations, sectors, and demographics: among them are positions of leadership, chances for learning and growth, and a sense of meaning at work. The fundamental requirements of income and benefits are at the bottom of what some scholars refer to as a "hierarchy of engagement," followed by possibilities for professional growth and advancement.

The second crucial factor in leadership is whether a leader fosters a sense of respect among their workforce. Alignment of values and meaning, which experts define as "a real sense of connection, a common purpose, and a shared sense of meaning at work," is the ultimate motivator of engagement. When it comes to what motivates employee engagement, there is no absolute rule. Regardless of the size or breadth of an organisation, it is obvious that effective leadership, growth opportunities, and the ability to participate in a meaningful vision are essential to inspiring people.

It's easy to forget our motivations in the midst of the daily grind. But it's imperative for managers to provide their employee more than a standard 9-to-5 job if they want to keep them motivated. One fact emerged loud and clear from the 560 respondents to Deloitte's Talent 2020 report: "Engage workers with meaningful work-or watch them walk out the door."

Being engaged at work is impossible if the task you are doing is not interesting. 42% of poll participants looking for new jobs said they felt their present position did not effectively utilise their talents and abilities. The findings of such surveys have been consistent. They discovered that employers who can discover the key to what gives work purpose will also discover the secret to employee engagement. Regardless of their age, sex, location, or term of employment, 55% of respondents felt that if they were engaged in meaningful work, their motivation levels would rise. 42% of people claimed they would be more devoted to their employer. More than one-third of respondents claimed they would take greater pleasure in their work and be prepared to spend longer hours to make sure the task was done.

Employers that want to instil a feeling of purpose in their workforce must have a distinct future vision. In fact, 77% of workers polled in the annual employee Job Happiness and Engagement study conducted by the Society for Human Resource Management stated having a clear knowledge of their organisation's vision and goals was crucial for their job satisfaction and engagement. employees are more likely to desire to contribute to a leader's vision if it is communicated to them clearly. HR professionals may use onboarding tools and elearning modules to spread this vision to workers at a large scale, ensuring that everyone is on the same page with an organisation's goals and ambitions from day one.

Leaders are all too frequently slowed down by repetitive and time-consuming administrative activities that are process-driven. Because of this, 75% of hiring managers and recruiters utilise application tracking or recruiting software to streamline the hiring procedure. Automating monotonous tasks is a good idea, so don't be hesitant to use technology. For instance, contemporary personnel management technology may assist you with anything from onboarding new employees to monitoring their continuing professional development activities and goals. It could free up your time so you can spend more time introducing them to new prospects and suggesting the resources and training they need to be effective in their position.

It should come as no surprise that senior leadership behaviour directly affects employee engagement. Leaders are key in giving your team a sense of purpose since they are the change-makers. As a result, it's critical that team leaders keep their word and implement real changes in response to any criticism.

Develop a strategy to put these changes into action after conducting a 360-degree feedback process to gain a sounding board for the problems in your organisation. In response to their comments, employees will evaluate their managers based on what they do, not what they say.

Your current workforce provides valuable insight into the efficacy of your HR management strategies. Look closely at your employee turnover rates because it's a good indicator of whether or not your employees are motivated to do their jobs. Any attrition rate above 10% points to an issue with your internal procedures. As soon as you can, think about conducting an employee engagement survey to identify your shortcomings and determine how to make adjustments.

What difference does it make how many hours your employees spend at work? Becoming outcomes-focused places greater emphasis on the results as long as the task is delivered on schedule and to the agreed-upon level. This strategy transfers accountability to workers while empowering them to operate in a way that suits their own requirements and way of life, increasing engagement.

In fact, a Harvard Business Review study found that businesses that gave workers greater flexibility in how they worked grew significantly while lowering turnover. Letting individuals work when they are most productive allows you to concentrate on evaluating the calibre of the job. This is true whether they finish early to pick up the kids from school or log back on late at night once the kids are in bed.

We frequently hear about the need to tailor the "employee work experience" to each individual. Given your organisation's organisational structure, that may be difficult. However, to genuinely understand each employee's preferred method of communication and then to use it is one thing that can be done. Adapt your communication approach to their preferred channel. Instead of forcing people to alter their behaviour, this will be more successful. You must put some effort into tailoring their experience if you really want to. Find out their preferred method of learning, and then design the learning opportunities to suit it. Because you demonstrated that you paid attention to what they said, seeing you adjust to their ways should improve their involvement.

Once an individual has received role-specific training, their growth shouldn't end. To keep workers interested, they must be continually pushed and upskilled at work. It's not necessary for this development to serve as directive instruction. Adopt a comprehensive approach to professional development by letting employees refine their talents in the ways they learn best, such as through visiting conferences, meetings, and hackathons. The goal is to provide employees with the resources and chances for self-directed growth rather than strict learning opportunities.

According to a recent SHRM poll, 67% of respondents evaluated respectful treatment of all employees at all levels as one of the most significant factors influencing workplace engagement and satisfaction. According to this research, HR professionals may expect better levels of engagement from their employees by building a working atmosphere that promotes communication, respect for others, and cooperation among workers at all levels.

Giving workers meaningful work and fostering an atmosphere where they may feel engagement on a regular basis are both important components of engaging employees. It will be difficult for any employee reporting to your organisation's managers to remain engaged if they don't care deeply about their employees aren't invested in their job. Leaders should set an example for their employee by putting as much enthusiasm and drive into their jobs as they do into their personal lives.

By establishing distinct leadership pipelines, you can demonstrate to employees your interest in their growth and future with the organisation. employee engagement in their roles depends on them feeling like they are heading someplace when there is a succession plan in place. A lack of professional advancement was reported as the main reason for leaving the organisation by 37% of employees changing positions in Deloitte's Talent 2020 series, which polled over 500 employees globally.

Whether a person feels interested in their position has a significant impact on whether things get off to a good start. In fact, if a new employee has a great first impression, they are more likely to stay with your organisation for longer than three years—close to 60% more likely. Engage employees before their first day of work with onboarding that gets them up to speed before they ever enter the building. employees learn how to perform their jobs effectively during onboarding and training, which also gives them a crucial opportunity to interact with you, clear up any uncertainties, and ask questions.

You're not alone if formal leadership pipelines are lacking in your organisation; many organisations face this challenge. According to a study, 53% of younger employees desire to hold leadership positions, but only 6% of organisations have effective leadership development initiatives in place to support this.

Increase proficiency more quickly using learning modules one of the most crucial things you can do to guarantee employees are engaged at work is to properly educate new personnel. You'll realise the expense of a comprehensive onboarding and learning regime pays for itself when you take into account that workers who can grasp their new responsibilities have a greater probability of accomplishing their goals and taking pleasure in what they do. Consider incorporating learning modules into your onboarding process to guide new hires through all of the required skill upskilling for their position, including critical (but time-consuming) compliance activities like Health and Safety training. For this, you may either employ pre-made learning curricula or develop your own learning modules especially designed for your business. By developing personalised learning curricula that describe your organisation's beliefs and objectives, you may also hasten a new hire's acquisition of cultural competence. This will not only make it easier for new hires to fit in with your business culture, but it will also encourage employer brand loyalty from the outset.

Utilise technology to offer ongoing educational opportunities One of the most effective tools an organisation can use to engage and grow its workforce is technology. employees may now take charge of their own learning in a variety of ways. Learning doesn't just have to take place during seminars or training days; it can also happen through podcasts, TED lectures, webinars, and online courses. According to Deloitte's research on human capital trends, learning opportunities are more than just a method to prepare employees for new responsibilities. In the research, it is said that "learning opportunities are among the greatest drivers of employee engagement and excellent workplace culture; they are part of the complete employee value offer, not only a method to acquire skills."

Never presume that money brings purpose. Don't think that giving employees a gift would make them feel appreciated. employees will feel much more appreciated in your organisation if you invest in their talent development rather than just giving them bonuses. Establish a work atmosphere that encourages challenge, fun, and skill growth. This is really helpful in conveying your concern for and regard for your workforce. Investing in learning and development provides employees with crucial buy-in for their future with your organisation, whether it is sending employees to conferences or helping them enhance their abilities and conduct training inside.

This creates ongoing difficulties. People need to feel like they can celebrate their own triumphs, despite the fact that many workers want a feeling of community at work. Nearly half of the respondents in a recent poll that sought to discover the factors influencing employee engagement indicated they found significance in their feelings of personal accomplishment and thrived under personal challenge. Make a list of your top performers and give them weekly, monthly, or annual challenges. These can be cultural, such as developing a new professional connection each week, or performance-driven, such as increasing KPIs or sales objectives.

By giving your employee networking opportunities, you may encourage them to bring new perspectives and best practise information to the office. Additionally, it strengthens the notion that they are respected inside the organisation. Share information about your employee with official and informal networks both inside and outside of the organisation. Ideas include hosting internal hackathons, sending selected employee to trade shows or conferences, and bringing teams from various departments together for a lunch meeting. Don't underestimate the influence social networks have on boosting workers' levels of job engagement. By having access to social networks like LinkedIn, Twitter, Slack, or Yammer, individuals may instantly assist one another in knowledge sharing and issue solving. This improves both the capacity to develop solid professional connections and overall job happiness.

It's time to retire outdated engagement tactics. Nowadays, businesses employ a wide range of full-time, part-time, contingent, contract, and flexible workers. A full-time employee's motivation will be very different from that of a freelancer. Instead of approaching people management with a one-size-fits-all philosophy, segment and customise talent management solutions to match people's various work styles. Instead of thinking of it as a permanent workforce, a proactive leader may consider it a virtual talent storehouse. Indeed, some of this talent may be "permanent," but a lot of it may be task-or project-based, hired to complete specific tasks. Perhaps not all of this skill is even human.

Don't merely hire for expertise and skill if you want to create teams of engaged workers. Make sure the people you hire have the right mindset and connect with your beliefs. One of the most crucial factors in keeping exceptional employees is cultural fit; workers who don't feel at home in their new position frequently depart within the first year. Up to 73% of professionals participating in a recent poll acknowledged quitting a job because of a bad cultural fit. It is obvious that doing things well the first time pays off when you consider the cost of turnover, which ranges from 50 to 60% of that employee's income.

It's crucial to hire for attitude and behaviour since the greatest outcomes aren't usually produced by the individual with the highest level of qualifications. To find people who aren't in the correct state of mind to offer value, look within your organisation. Sometimes all it takes is finding this team member a position that better utilises their skills. If you are unable to find this person a position within your organisation, it may be time to have a serious discussion with them:

Although creating an atmosphere that encourages deeper employee involvement requires dedication, grit, and guts, the outcomes will be great for both your employees and your organisation. Integrating a "courageous atmosphere" is a great strategy to support organisational ideals, cultural diversity, and authenticity. It is important to accept and value everyone's viewpoints in order to ultimately foster an atmosphere in which individuals may flourish. It is important to create an empowering symbol, such as a "Courage Coin," that may be used to remove any obstacles (real or imagined) and to promote timely, open communication. Explain the proper conduct for using the coin: be courteous, on-task, and receptive to the presenter's ideas. The person who is delivering this symbol is being brave; pay attention to what they have to say and avoid interrupting or becoming defensive. Additionally, express gratitude for the person's insights.

It's crucial to create flexible, cross-functional teams in the modern global economy so they can react quickly to market developments. This mobility is not only essential for organisations who are looking to the future, but it is also a fundamental strategy for increasing employee engagement. Collaboration is crucial for workers to feel included and involved. According to studies, teams with a cross-functional mindset, shared leadership duties, and interpersonal connections had lower levels of stress and conflict and better levels of overall happiness.

Not just leaders and managers are accountable for employee engagement. All employees within an organisation play a crucial role in ensuring that everyone is an active and valuable team member. In fact, 70% of respondents to SHRM's employee Job Satisfaction and Engagement Report rated having a workplace that encourages employees to engage pro-actively when they spot a problem or opportunity as very important. Another 65% of respondents gave high priority to coworkers who could swiftly adjust to problems or emergency situations as well as those who persisted in the face of obstacles at work. In order to promote cross-functional cooperation, internal silos must be broken down and traditional hierarchical team structures must be abandoned. The concept that anybody in the organisation, regardless of seniority or tenure, may contribute their talents to an issue is fundamental to cross-functionality.

These statistics highlight how crucial it is for workers to believe they are part of a team that is resilient, adaptable, and goal-focused. The promotion of a collaborative and problem-solving culture encourages employee to think creatively and work out issues within their teams instead of relying on management's direction.

To foster a sense of involvement at work, it is essential to build strong relationships with coworkers. Being social animals who frequently spend more time with our coworkers than with our friends and family, it comes naturally to want to interact with folks in our immediate environment.

According to research, an employee's psychological sense of purpose at work is directly influenced by the relationships they have with their coworkers and managers.

To encourage employee engagement and motivation at work, a sense of personal significance and participation in a team are essential. According to research, two out of every five employees believe that their connections with their coworkers are crucial to their fulfilment.

Encourage business activities that involve employees engaging and working together often; this fosters a sense of belonging and a common goal. Daily practises like team standups, cross-team communication tools like Slack and Trello, and business outings like bootcamps and vacations are a few examples.

If giving work a purpose is essential to keeping people motivated, you should think of methods to enhance the value of each function beyond merely fulfilling your organisation's objectives. Adopt a comprehensive strategy that recognises the value of social responsibility in the workplace and in life. Give workers the option to support the community via their employment in big or little ways, such as by organising a charity fun run or organising charity activities that the entire manpower may participate in. A recent poll of companies that provide workers the option to improve society via their job revealed that over one-third of respondents felt the opportunity made their present employment feel more important. Over-55s cherish this opportunity in particular.

In today's workplace, having a strong sense of ethics and corporate culture is more than just great to have. According to one survey, 90% of professionals explore a organisation's culture before taking a position, which is why it's critical to be adamant about your organisation's values.

If people managers want to recruit a younger workforce that prioritises ethics over career advancement opportunities, they must develop a clear set of values. In reality, the importance of values fit for employees is rising; in a poll, 14% of participants said that their current employer's values were a major factor in their decision to work there.

Make encouraging innovation a high priority in your management plan, and you'll keep employees interested every day. Include a creative code in your organisation's timesheet policy if it is required, and aggressively encourage employees to utilise it. Gameify brainstorming sessions. Encourage your workers to use whatever tool the workplace has available to spark an idea or start a business.There are innovative individuals in every organisation, and they ought to be supported. However, there is a significant difference between encouraging the occasional out-of-the-box thought and encouraging creativity as a method of conducting business.

Give workers an opportunity to contribute to the organisation's overall success. According to a research on employee engagement done by the Penna Institute, the chance to contribute to the organisation's success is one of the top three elements that influences employee engagement. In the survey, over half of the respondents stated that having the chance to help the organisation succeed led to a fulfilling work experience that facilitated personal growth and job satisfaction.

Avoid using a one-size-fits-all strategy. Depending on their generation, workers assign various elements differing degrees of importance. Studies have revealed, for instance, that millennials value job growth chances more than baby boomers do. In a similar vein, Generation Xers may find that an organisation's dedication to professional growth gives them more happiness than Baby Boomers do. This means that you should strive to adjust to each employee's requirements and incentives as much as possible, rather than taking a uniform approach to talent management. HR practitioners need to be aware of the elements that motivate workers from different generations as the baby boomer generation retires and the workforce demographics change.

Here's a super easy trick that works really well: Encourage your managers to make it a point to express gratitude to one person or team every day until it becomes routine for the organisation. It's so simple to overlook the positive and be quick to criticise. Be the location that honours and celebrates achievement. Small celebrations on a regular basis are preferable to making a big deal out of it once in a blue moon. The employee acknowledgement for their efforts and the fact that several of them went above and beyond is much appreciated by the employee.

employee motivation will increase by combining these elements into a personalised experience. organisations should try to rethink performance management such that constant feedback, acknowledgment, and development become the guiding principles rather than do away with performance evaluations altogether. employee engagement will be boosted by combining these elements into a personalised experience.

Integrating pulse performance concepts into daily operations to promote frequent feedback, constant dialogue, and agile alignment to goals rather than judging previous performance, investing in leadership development by teaching managers on how to provide feedback and "what has to be done next" using a variety of sources to gather and analyse information about a worker's performance and develop a more comprehensive viewpoint.

Consider involving employees in a more informal feedback loop rather than depending just on the dreaded annual performance review. The performance review process can be portrayed as a friendly, collaborative event rather than a personal assessment by removing its formality. People Leaders who want to maintain employee engagement throughout the year can think about incorporating performance dialogues into routine tasks. This can be done through unofficial one-on-one meetings, regular stand-up meetings, or on-the-spot mentoring and feedback. Good work should not just be acknowledged by management.

Go over and offer your sincere congratulations to the person when you learn about their accomplishment. When you achieve huge victories, it will mean a lot to that individual, and they'll probably feel the same way about you. If a portion of your team works remotely, turning on employee recognition software may greatly increase virtual employee engagement and make it simple to celebrate coworkers even when you can't visit them at their desk in person. A good manager is necessary for an engaged team. On National Boss's Day, we all honour good managers since they enhance morale and prevent high turnover. We are aware that motivating your employee may feel like an impossible chore that you will never complete.

"Making growth opportunities available to people who desire them is the best strategy."

An organisation need not be a non-profit or social enterprise to foster an environment where millennial employees feel their job matters. Technology has greatly empowered millennials, as it has all of us in general. They like staying connected online through both personal and business networks since they are social media savvy and cooperative. Therefore, it is excellent to engage on these platforms and develop interactive experiences with clear expectations given forth by the employer on the opportunity, the deliverables, and the what's-in-it-for-me. LinkedIn, Facebook Jobs, and online review sites like Glassdoor are popular places to find and recruit millennials. Other well-known job sites where employers can find excellent full-time and freelance millennial talent include Naukri, Shine, Indeed, Hirist.com, Angel List, Freshersworld, iimjobs.com, and freelancing markets like Upwork.com.

An organisation's biggest asset is its employees. Whether the product is a vehicle or a cosmetic has no bearing. A business is only as good as the employees it retains. employees are an intangible and dynamic asset, as opposed to tangible and physical assets like machinery, plants, and equipment. Higher productivity, lower customer turnover, and improved brand recognition across internal and external audiences are all guaranteed for businesses with motivated employees who emotionally connect to their job.

Aligning employees' personal aspirations with the larger corporate and strategic goals of the organisation is essential for any organisation to have sustainable development and success. A strong performance management procedure may be implemented to achieve this. The groundwork for establishing a conversational culture inside an organisation is laid forth by a well-defined and well-implemented Corporate Performance Management (CPM) procedure. Simply defined, it promotes open communication between employees and management, ensuring that everyone is on the same page.

Millennials are frequently referred to as the generation of quick gratification, whether this is accurate or not. organisations can enable a customised employee experience based on the nature of the work by supplying the necessary tools and making necessary policy changes. This includes flexible work for employees who want to work independently and standard working hours when they must work collaboratively in groups. You must be mindful of the fact that the gig economy is preferred by the niche-skilled workforce and that 92% of millennials prioritise flexibility when looking for work. They select recruiting practises such as responsiveness, quick feedback, and mobile-and technology-friendly job sites. Nurture oftentimes, what is regarded as "millennial entitlement" is a desire for development and advancement.

"Employers that are effectively linking their social missions to their employee's daily work are differentiating themselves in the market and generating big returns. Taking the necessary steps to ensure every employee knows how they fulfill the mission, achieve the vision, and execute one or more organisational strategies through his or her daily job really pays off." - Tamar Elkeles

According to studies, millennials are substantially more receptive to learning and entrepreneurship than previous generations. They frequently look for learning and professional development options that will enable them to advance in their jobs as well as experiment with and pursue horizontal ones. Give them difficult tasks, give internal talent mobility top attention, and make sure they have the necessary independence in their job. Giving them more control equates to releasing their power. They keep putting their best foot forward via ongoing learning and professional advancement. Every organisation ought to make an effort to adopt a disciplined strategy in this regard.

I'm constantly reminded to start with the end in mind, which is the second habit established by Stephen Covey in his best-selling book "The 7 Habits of Highly Effective People," whenever I embark on a new project. What individuals must have the potential to achieve or become as a result of participation in such a program when you develop a top talent program to find those who have it. How will they help your business achieve its goals once their potential has been realised? How about managing force reductions and restructuring, developing new goods, or developing into authorities in their fields? These questions will help you determine the kind of potential you want to discover and nurture.

In your opinion, which skill sets are the most crucial for an individual to reenter the workforce?

When we think about talent, we take into account a number of factors, including how to access it, how to acquire it, how to develop talent, and how to assist others in realising their full potential. No matter who we are, the most crucial quality we want is the capacity for learning, or learning agility. We acknowledge that, despite the fact that any organisation may employ someone for a certain set of talents, the pace of change and the need for abilities is fairly quick. It is essential to upgrade your skills or make sure you maintain them if you want to return to employment. Particularly since the epidemic, the requirement for competent workers has grown indisputable. Not to mention the ongoing engagement and investment that organisations make in the skilling, re-skilling, and upskilling of their workforce.

"In a competitive job market, making the effort to address skill gaps shows desire and provides employees with a competitive edge over others."

Competitive workplaces can produce stress, and intense, relentless expectations can result in burnout, a debilitating illness. Additionally, this also applies to leaders. Leaders typically have busy schedules, and throughout the daily grind, self-care frequently gets neglected.

What easy self-care techniques can leaders utilise to regain lost energy even on their busiest days?

Prioritising your health is the best practise . We advise people to modify their viewpoint in order to identify the components of their condition that are irreversible and those that are changeable, restrict their exposure to the most demanding activities and people, and look for supportive social networks.

Make time for your friends, get adequate sleep, prioritise eating well, and balance work and play in your calendar. Additionally, self-pampering is a straightforward but sometimes neglected type of self-care.

Flexible or agile HR is an iterative development process that relies on experimentation, integration, and evaluation and is supported by a collaborative and trusting culture. Although agile's roots are in software development, it is now being applied more and more in the field of human resources.

"Agile is an approach used in the HR industry that frequently puts responsiveness and adaptability first."

employee involvement is ensured through the collection of employee feedback and the bottom-up development of many of our HR policies and procedures. You were constantly conscious of the need to adapt certain procedures in order to integrate an agile method of working into HR business operations. For instance, one of the first things you might have altered, for instance, was the way you did employee surveys. Once a year, you might be doing a typical survey with a consulting organisation, and the respondents may be slow to react. Today, you need quick feedback if you want to be nimble.

Any organisation plan might be modified. As a result, HR managers need to anticipate effectively and actively monitor existing developments. These patterns aid in your analysis of impending changes and how the business will have to modify its existing strategy to address the new environment. To obtain more useful insights, you might choose a certain approach or combine many strategies. However, the following sorts of data must be accessible and updated for all types of forecasting systems:

- The future productivity of an organisation is directly impacted by its existing talent pool and its anticipated future talent pool.
- HR metrics give HR executives the information they need to assess the organisation's resource management practises. These measurements also assist HR management in determining how much money will need to be spent in the future to meet projected labour demands.
- Forecasts of HR needs may cover a period of up to five years. Technical HR estimates won't be very useful in five years because of evolving technology and

unpredictability.

- Understanding competitors' corporate cultures and benefit offerings is one of the data sources for competitor analysis.

In order to adjust any factors that could be impeding the results, HR management must continuously analyse and monitor the strategic workforce plan's success during the implementation phase.

employee turnover may be predicted early on by looking at the absence rate. A high absenteeism rate provides insight into how many workers would be let go or how many would need to be employed to make up for the productivity gap caused by absence when predicting future workforce demand.

Further, the turnover rate aids HR executives in estimating the number of replacements required over the next few years. employees' voluntary resignations and the total number of layoffs from the previous year are included in turnover. This information paints a general picture of the situation of employees today and calls for more investigation.

Additionally, you need to be able to react promptly to criticism. You might have used agility for your goal-setting procedures as well. To encourage better responsibility and concentration, which are closely related to skill development and incentives, you may introduce quarterly goal setting at the team and individual levels. The manager serves as a facilitator in your employee development plan, which is a bilateral process where individuals are responsible for defining their careers. In order to plan their career's next steps, employees create development objectives in addition to business goals based on their priorities.

It's critical to concentrate on filling essential roles first since these roles call for specialised talents that are hard to find, making applicants competitive in the job market. As a result, filling critical roles could take longer, and business operations might be adversely affected if they remain unfilled for an extended period of time.

"In the majority of sectors, it is now feasible to purchase machinery and equipment on the worldwide market that is equivalent to that used by the top multinational corporations. The deciding element is not having access to tools and machines. Effectiveness is in using it."
- Dr. Amit Das

References

- *HR Disrupted: It's Time for Something Different by Lucy Adams*
- *Thinking, Fast and Slow by Daniel Kahneman*
- *Nine Lies About Work: A Freethinking Leader's Guide to the Real World by Marcus Buckingham, Ashley Goodall*
- *How to Win Friends and Influence People by Dale Carnegie*
- *HR Rising!!: From Ownership to Leadership by Steve Browne*
- *Belonging at Work: Everyday Actions You Can Take to Cultivate an Inclusive Organization by Rhodes Perry, MPA*
- *People Processes: How Your People Can Be Your Organization's Competitive Advantage Hardcover – Import, 11 September 2018 by Rhamy Alejeal.*
- *The Fearless Organization: Creating Psychological Safety in the Workplace for Learning, Innovation, and Growth by Amy C. Edmondson*
- *The Practical Guide to HR Analytics: Using Data to Inform, Transform, and Empower HR Decisions by Shonna D. Waters, Valerie N. Streets, Lindsay McFarlane, and Rachael Johnson-Murray*
- *Strategic Human Resource Management: An HR Professional's Toolkit by Karen Beaven*
- *The Resource Management and Capacity Planning Handbook, A Guide to Maximizing the Value of Your Limited People Resources by Jerry Manas, 2014*
- *Predictive HR Analytics: Mastering the HR Metric by Kirsten & Martin Edwards, 2017*
- *Victory Through Organization by Dave Ulrich, David*

REFERENCES

Kryscynski, Wayne Brockbank, Mike Ulrich, 2013

- *The HR Scorecard by Brian Becker, Mark Huselid, Dave Ulrich, 2015*
- *HR from the Outside In: Six Competencies for the Future of Human Resources by Dave Ulrich, Jon Younger, Wayne Brockbank, Mike Ulrich, 2011*
- *Human Resource Management By Gary Dessler, 2016*
- *Investing in people. Financial Impact of Human Resource Initiatives by KirsWayne Cascio, John Boudreau*
- *The Talent Delusion by Tomas Chamorro-Premuzic*
- *Work Rules! by Laszlo Bock*
- *Human Resources Administration in Education-A Management Approach by Ronald W. Rebore, 2010*
- *HBR's 10 Must Reads on Reinventing HR, Harvard Business Review by Marcus Buckingham Reid Hoffman · Ram Charan Peter Cappelli, Dec 2019*
- *The Chief HR Officer: Defining the New Role of Human Resource Leaders Hardcover by Patrick M. Wright (Editor), John W. Boudreau (Editor), David Pace (Editor), Elizabeth Sartain (Editor), Paul McKinnon (Editor), Richard L. Antoine (Editor), May 2011*
- *HR Transformation: Building Human Resources From the Outside In by Dave Ulrich, Wayne Brockbank, Jon Younger, Mark Nyman, Justin Allen , August 2009*
- *Human Resource Management By Gary Dessler, Biju Varrkey, December 2017*
- *The Big Book of HR: Updated Edition Paperback by Carnelia Gamlem, Barbara Mitchell, December 2017*
- *Sultan Chand & Son's Human Resource Management by L. M. Prasad, January 2018*
- *The New HR Leader's First 100 Days: How To Start Strong, Hit The Ground Running & Achieve Success Faster by Alan Collins November, 2017*

REFERENCES

- *The Resource Management and Capacity Planning Handbook A Guide to Maximizing the Value of Your Limited People Resources by Jerry Manas, 2014*
- *Peace at Work: The HR Manager's Guide to Workplace by John Ford September, 2014*
- *The Principal as Human Resources Leader: A Guide to Exemplary Practices for Personnel Administration (Eye on Education Books) 1st Edition by M. Scott Norton, Jan 2014*
- *Understanding and Managing Diversity: Readings, Cases, and Exercises 6th Edition by Carol Harvey , M. June Allard , 2014*
- *Talent, Transformation, and the Triple Bottom Line, How Companies Can Leverage Human Resources to Achieve Sustainable Growth by Andrew W. Savitz, Karl Weber, Edward E. Lawler, 2013*
- *Human Resource Management by Raymond Noe, John Hollenbeck, Barry Gerhart, Patrick Wright, 2020*
- *Human Resource Management, People, Data, and Analytics by Talya Bauer, Berrin Erdogan, David E. Caughlin, Donald M. Truxillo, 2019*
- *Carrots and Sticks Don't Work ,Build a Culture of Employee Engagement with the Principles of Respect by Paul L. Marciano, 2010*
- *Fundamentals of Human Resource Management by Raymond Noe, John Hollenbeck, Barry Gerhart, Patrick Wright, 2019*
- *Human Resource Selection by Robert Gatewood, Hubert S. Feild, Murray Barrick, 2015*
- *Human Resource Management by Robert L. Mathis, John H. Jackson, Sean R. Valentine, Patricia Meglich, 2016*
- *The Essential HR Handbook, 10th Anniversary Edition, A Quick and Handy Resource for Any Manager or HR Professional by Sharon Armstrong, Barbara Mitchell, 2019*

REFERENCES

- *101 Tough Conversations to Have With Employees, A Manager's Guide To Addressing Performance, Conduct, And Discipline Challenges by Paul Falcone. 2019*

About The Author

Dr. Amit Das, is a renowned executive advisor, consultant, educationist, author, speaker, counsellor, and coach whose 25+ years of business experience provides high-impact, practical solutions that support his clients' leadership development and organisational transformations. He worked for fortune 500 MNCs and left rich leagacy of organising transformational learning workshops. He has transformed more than 5000+ working executives through his path breaking capability building learning workshops. Dr. Amit Das is recognised as an innovative, principled thought leader who combines intellectual rigor and discipline with an ability to translate theory into practice. His operational skills are coupled with a strategic ability to analyse, develop, and implement successful strategies for profitability, growth, and sustainability.

Dr. Amit Das has a successful track record in aligning learning and training solutions to key business strategy with a strong focus on flawless execution excellence to facilitate individual, business divisional, and organisational performance. He keeps relentless focus on measuring training impact and ROI, people capability building graphs, training process governance, performance coaching, and strategic thinking. These have been some of his key individual success traits. His core capabilities include performance coaching, designing training and development frameworks, psychometric assessment and analysis, competency framework development and assessments, content design and facilitation of soft skills and leadership programmes, Learning Management Systems, Learning Impact Measurement, Talent Analysis, and Performance Coaching and Counselling.

ABOUT THE AUTHOR

Dr. Amit Das has authored multiple management and self-development books, like Create Your Leadership Edge, Love-Laugh- Live With Happiness, SMART Parenting @ Zero Cost, Building Organisational Capability, Ethical Road Map, Attomic Attention, BYPB, Redefining The Power Of Mentoring, Making The Most Future Fit Organisation, Redefining Talent Management, Defining Your Success Factors, Lead or Plead, Make The Most Of Your Life, Better Half or Bitter Half, Psychology Of Learning And Development, The Transformative Mind & Soul are few of them.

He has a Ph.D. and a Fellowship in strategic learning, along with his first class degrees in Human Resource Management, Marketing Management, International Business, and Corporate Laws from the top business schools in India. He is a certified Psychometric analyst, HR Analyst, OD Interventionist, Human Psychologist, Lifecoach, Leadership Developer, Black Belt (LSS), Strategic Thinker, Talent Analyst, certified professional trainer from the U.K. and certified behavioral coach from the U.S.A.

Dr. Amit Das likes googling, reading books, writing articles & books, cooking, listening to old melodies, and counselling people to unleash their true potential to build a strong nation. He is married and blessed with a son. He would love to hear about your experience after reading his books. You can email him and share your thoughts, or you can use his services for life coaching, positive behavioural counseling, educational support, and mentoring for young, promising students pursuing their B.B.A. and M.B.A. degrees.